T0311341

SMART CAREER MOVES
FOR SMART WOMEN

Written for the businesswoman and professional, this book offers insights and guidance on making the right decisions about career paths and shows ways to strategically prepare for a career transition, be it a promotion, change of sector, setting up one's own business, or even changing careers altogether.

Women are looking more and more at a change of work set-up (to 'at home' and hybrid models) and what they want out of their careers and wider life. In easy-to-follow steps, this book demystifies the unwritten rules of making a successful career transition. The reader is provided with a highly practical guide to navigating professional changes at all career points and of all types – as well as a toolkit to facilitate the practice of these new skills and approaches. The book encourages professional women to stop, reflect, and do the groundwork on where they want their career to go. It provides the tools to identify what they want, prepare for change, and cultivate the necessary skills and self-confidence key to a successful career transition.

The insights and actionable steps contained in this book make it an invaluable resource for professional women looking to achieve success and navigate the transitional stages of their career, re-enter the workplace after a career break, or who simply want to develop the tools and skills to make smart career moves.

Susan Doering is an international career and leadership coach who operates globally, coaching individuals to achieve professional success and facilitating career development training courses for private and public sector organisations.

"It's important for women to build a list of 'trusted advisors' along with a corporate career survival tool kit, for which *Smart Career Moves for Smart Women* is invaluable! A successful career is more than just skills, it's important to take control of your career from the outset, ensuring that you are clear about your values, so that any career decision you make is values led – this book creates the framework to allow you to do this! I wish this book had been available when I started my career, more than 40 years ago."

Dr. Heather Melville OBE, *Senior Managing Director, Teneo*

"This book reveals the hidden skills necessary to be successful in moving between different work environments and how to be flexible while staying true to your core values and passion."

Dr. Sama Bilbao y Leon, *Director General, World Nuclear Association*

"At a time of rapid, global change in society and the marketplace, women, especially, need to learn to adapt and prepare for their next career move, and this book is the ideal companion which shows how to do that."

Kirsty Gogan, *Managing Director, Lucid Catalyst*

"Susan has been a fabulous coach and professional resource with immense skill in helping one navigate career development. The book will be a great help to many professional women wanting insights and practical steps for developing their career."

Dr. Liz Williams, *Board Director, National Computational Infrastructure (NCI), Australia*

"A subject that is very close to my heart has been handled here by an experienced career coach with sensitivity and understanding of the challenges professional women face."

Cornelia von Rittberg, *Business Matchmaker & Regenerator; International Art Broker*

"A wealth of insight and strategies offered with a personal tone and style that feels like Susan is coaching you along toward your goals."

Jan M. Walton, *Human Resources and Organisational Change Consultant*

"Dr Doering has written a practical, focussed guide for any woman struggling with the complex and challenging issues around career transition. Real-life examples bring the issues to life, and Dr Doering's compassionate, coaching-focussed advice would be an invaluable resource for any professional woman at a career crossroads. The text shows a deep and helpful understanding of the issues facing women thinking about a career change. Dr Doering's wide professional expertise and understanding of different cultural contexts give the book wide relevance."

Susan le Jeune d'Allegeershecque CBE, *Secretary General, International Order of St John of Jerusalem*

"Transitioning into a new role can undermine confidence and be extremely stressful if not approached in a pro-active way. Susan guides the reader through the balancing act of establishing credibility, building relationships and delivering on expectations."

Helen Isacke, *Founder and Director, Trusted Coach Directory UK*

"*Smart Career Moves for Smart Women* is essential reading for women at all stages in their career, and one that they can return to again and again as they encounter or seek new transitions.

Written in a clear, honest and straight-talking style, it offers meaningful insights that will resonate with all working women. Having already made one major career transition with a change of both sectors and roles, a lot of the themes feel personally applicable. I am now finding myself returning to Susan's insights as I embark on motherhood and the inevitable transition this will entail for my career. I will definitely be consulting this book when I contemplate how I want to re-enter working life after maternity leave and how I want to shape my career around my shifting values and needs.

Susan masterfully applies her own expertise and emotional intelligence to sometimes complex situations and gives actionable advice that will give the reader the confidence and clarity of thought to grapple with the essential questions all women need to ask themselves about the outcomes they are seeking and what they are willing and able to change to make these happen. The toolkits and journaling exercises are excellent and will allow readers to engage with the content as actively as they choose and offer great value to return to again and again.

The content is particularly timely and relevant as we adjust to the new 'post-pandemic reality' where women (and men) have realised a level of flexibility and work-life balance that can produce better outcomes for both their productivity and their well-being.

I will certainly be consulting this book often as I navigate new changes and challenges in my career and transitions I wish to make. The valuable insight and advice it provides for women at all stages of their careers and across sectors makes it an unmissable read."

Katie Reading, *Wine Buyer*

SMART CAREER MOVES FOR SMART WOMEN

HOW TO SUCCEED IN CAREER TRANSITIONS

Susan Doering

Routledge
Taylor & Francis Group

LONDON AND NEW YORK

Designed cover image: Adam Renvoize

First published 2023
by Routledge
4 Park Square, Milton Park, Abingdon, Oxon OX14 4RN

and by Routledge
605 Third Avenue, New York, NY 10158

Routledge is an imprint of the Taylor & Francis Group, an informa business

British Library Cataloguing-in-Publication Data
A catalogue record for this book is available from the British Library

Library of Congress Cataloging-in-Publication Data
Names: Doering, Susan (Career transition coach), author.
Title: Smart career moves for smart women : how to succeed in career transitions / Susan Doering.
Description: Abingdon, Oxon ; New York, NY : Routledge, 2023. | Includes bibliographical references and index.
Identifiers: LCCN 2022041184 (print) | LCCN 2022041185 (ebook) | ISBN 9781032404417 (hardback) | ISBN 9781032404356 (paperback) | ISBN 9781003353720 (ebook)
Subjects: LCSH: Women—Vocational guidance. | Career development. | Career changes. | Work-life balance.
Classification: LCC HF5382.6 .D64 2023 (print) | LCC HF5382.6 (ebook) | DDC 650.1082—dc23/eng/20220902
LC record available at https://lccn.loc.gov/2022041184
LC ebook record available at https://lccn.loc.gov/2022041185

ISBN: 978-1-032-40441-7 (hbk)
ISBN: 978-1-032-40435-6 (pbk)
ISBN: 978-1-003-35372-0 (ebk)

DOI: 10.4324/9781003353720

Typeset in Bembo
by codeMantra

To my sons, Stefan and Laurence

CONTENTS

ABOUT THE AUTHOR

Dr Susan Doering is an international career coach and executive leadership mentor. She has a coaching diploma and is a Professional Certified Coach accredited by the International Coaching Federation (ICF). She is also a Myers Briggs practitioner and is Resonance Coaching certified and holds a Master's degree from the University of Oxford and a PhD from the University of Vienna, Austria.

Susan has accompanied hundreds of clients in a variety of sectors across the globe in their quest for a fulfilling career. With a multinational outlook, she has coached in English, French, and German with a focus on women at a turning point in their lives.

Having transitioned herself from university lecturing to global event production and then again to executive training and coaching, she has had many lives building her career while nurturing her passions for music and literature and raising two sons.

Susan lives in London, where she is an active campaigner for diversity and inclusion, and environmental causes. She is also a keen gardener in her local community garden in Greenwich.

ACKNOWLEDGEMENTS
AND THANKS

My thanks go first to all the wonderful coaching clients I have had over the years who allowed me to travel alongside them in their journeys of career transitions. It is something of a leap of faith to entrust one's hopes and fears to an outsider, and I value the trust that they gave me. Their career journeys, from setting out with aspirations and hopes to navigating the hurdles met along the way, formed the basis for this book. Their perseverance and courage to overcome their challenges inspired me to collect the tools and reflections we used in the hope that they will empower more women.

I would like to thank all those friends who provided astute feedback on early iterations of the book, especially my dear friend Sally Reading, whose hawk-eye attention to grammatical detail, professional expertise, and personal experience enabled her to give the best possible advice. Thanks to Eva-Maria Volpe, who provided invaluable comments on the text and whose life experience was reflected in her profound understanding of what the female reader would need. My thanks go also to Tony Young, whose careful comments and insight challenged me to re-think and improve my book. Sincere thanks to the reviewers of the final draft for their suggestions, most of which have found their way into the final edit, and for their interest and enthusiasm for the topic.

My deepest thanks go to my freelance development editor, Louise Goulsbra, of Content Box UK, who has given me the most amazing support throughout as the midwife who helped this baby see the light of day. Louise was always there, never stinting in both encouragement and astute professional guidance. She made the road to publication not only possible but also hugely enjoyable.

Finally, I would like to thank Rebecca Marsh at Routledge, who recognised in the book a spark that could illuminate the career paths of readers, for which I am sincerely grateful.

PREFACE – MY PERSONAL STORY OF CAREER TRANSITIONS

My first real, full-time job after completing my PhD degree in Comparative Literature was a research and teaching post at the same university. However, I did not sufficiently realise that there is a difference between a job and a career and that I should invest thought and energy into developing my career as well as into the tasks that constituted my job. I was naïve about all the things you need to do to build up a professional reputation and shape your career. Although there were no immediate consequences in the early stages of my career, later it was clear that other (in the majority male) colleagues had overtaken me and that I was not going to have the same career opportunities in the academic world as them. This played out in a very real way after I married and had two children.

For a few years, I juggled teaching at the university part-time, trying to meet the demands of a university department head and a husband who felt I should really be a full-time wife and mother. In consequence, I gave up my university post to devote myself to my family. At the time, I did not have the self-confidence or the know-how to research alternative options, or to weigh up the pros and cons and craft a solution that would have better suited who I really was.

Being a full-time wife and mother of small children, however, did not satisfy my need for intellectual or social stimulus. I was doing translation work to keep the brain cells going when an opportunity arose through a friend who, as President of the World

Association of Psychotherapists, was planning a global conference in Vienna, where I was living at the time. He needed someone to plan and organise the social programme for the delegates and thought I might be interested. (I have since wondered whether the offer might partly have been made with his psychotherapist's hat on.)

As a former university teacher in German and Comparative Literature, I had no training or experience managing a project and practically no knowledge of planning or budgeting, but I grasped the idea enthusiastically with an open mind. I learned on the job, put in hundreds of unpaid hours (ah, yes… a common mistake) and made it a success.

So, I changed direction completely and for the next few years project managed three consecutive, large-scale projects: the social programme of the global conference, an international opera production at a music festival, and a classical music ensemble's performing and recording schedule.

During this transitionary time, I relied on some of the things I was good at, such as being outgoing and people-oriented, being multilingual, a fast learner, adaptable, hard-working, and fairly well organised. I learned how to work with different kinds of people and teams, and learned a lot about how to manage people, but I still felt like a square peg in a round hole as I did not have – and did not acquire – any formal training in project management.

My lack of formal training or qualifications in project management during these three projects was one obstacle, as was the fact that I was an outsider in the music world and lacked the network and visibility that I would really have needed to progress.

By now, my life had changed again as my sons had grown up and I was divorced. I was earning next to nothing, and I needed to put my life in order and find work which would provide an acceptable income.

I asked myself two questions: How much do I enjoy what I am doing at the moment, and what am I good at? I realised I quite enjoyed what I was doing but that I would have to invest in my know-how and credibility by getting some qualifications and in building up the right network to be really successful as a manager in the classical music industry – and I was not sure that I really wanted to do that.

So, I decided to reach out to my friends and acquaintances. Did they have any ideas or advice?

One friend in a large international organisation passed me on to a colleague, the head of their conferences department, who, after listening carefully to my qualifications and experience, said with great insight: 'It seems to me that what you're really good at is teaching. Let me put you in touch with the head of our training department.' The result was that I designed and delivered a diversity training course for managers of that organisation. This was not a subject I knew a lot about in theory or as a credential, but I had always been interested in diversity and gender balance at work and my research skills came in useful here. Planning a training course was also something I was very conversant with from my time as a university teacher.

It went well, and so began a new career phase – I was recommended to other international organisations in the same capacity and also received formal training in their programmes.

WHY DID THIS CAREER TRANSITION WORK?

I played to my strengths: research, teaching/training, working with groups of learners, giving presentations, and researching methodologies and subject matter. I was open to continually learning and adapting to the needs of those around me. Indeed, it was as I was beginning to take the first steps in my new career as a trainer that I realised there was scope to develop my role further. I noticed that participants in my training courses often shared with me the challenges they were experiencing at work, and I wanted to acquire the expertise to help them. I completed a professional coaching course to qualify with a diploma in Career and Executive Coaching, and coaching has since become central to my professional life.

Over time, I built up a network in the world of international organisations, especially for humanitarian organisations, and created visibility for myself as a coach and facilitator for specific programmes, including career development and career transitions. My work with the staff of international organisations in training and coaching programmes has been extremely rewarding and has spanned the last 14 years. This work aligns perfectly with my values of care, respect, diversity and inclusion, gender equality, independence, and freedom of choice.

WHAT HAVE I LEARNED ALONG THE WAY?

1. Lifelong learning is key. It is vital to be prepared to learn. In every career step, we will have to learn something new, such as an additional skill or something complementary to the skills already in our portfolio. Being continually open to learning new skills and acquiring new knowledge and insight will not only ensure we are ready for our next challenge when it presents itself but also allows us to grow as individuals, builds confidence, and ensures we can keep up with ever-evolving professional settings. And there is another reason why we should never give up learning: it keeps our brain active! This plays a large part in maintaining our alertness and our mental and even physical health; these are interconnected in ways that science has only now begun to comprehend.

2. Developing a level of self-awareness and understanding our values is central to making good decisions. We can only do this if we allow ourselves to take the time for self-reflection and not always just continue on the same path, but rather stop to ask ourselves: 'is this the path I want to take now?' One of the themes running through this book is finding out who you want to be, and it's important to recognise that that can change over time.

3. Career moves, whether they are a new position or an entirely new career path, force us to confront the challenges of the external world as well as our own doubts and fears; if we can identify what we are really good at and what really interests us, we can overcome those hurdles and move forward to become stronger, probably happier and more confident than before. If I had had the self-confidence to act on my real

interests and wishes, I would have sought a better solution for my career-life situation much earlier. I would also have realised that I needed to research more options and consider each one. For example, I see now that there was a point when I could have found my way back into an academic life if I had wanted to.

And this is why I have written this book. If I had read a book like this during the time I was struggling with deciding what to do in my life and with my career, I would have realised that I had choices and would have been much more intentional about carving out the work scenario I wanted and developing the skills I needed to make things happen.

That is the most empowering thought for all of us. We all have choices; we must simply shine a light on them and add a little intention to our decision-making and draw on some of the tools and techniques I will share with you. In the words of Shirley Chisholm: 'If they don't give you a seat at the table, bring a folding chair.'

Please note that the case studies used throughout the book are designed to illustrate the discussion points. They are based on scenarios Susan has worked with but all names and background information have been changed to protect anonymity.

INTRODUCTION – TAKING CONTROL OF YOUR CAREER

EMBRACING CHANGE

This book is about change in our professional lives. It examines how we can take charge of our careers, move more easily from one phase of our life to the next, and thrive in each one. It offers signposts, directions, support, and food for thought for the journey, and encourages you to look forward to and welcome the next stage. Wherever you are in your professional life, you can take stock and ask yourself: Where do I want to go next and how do I get there?

I believe it is important to talk specifically about career transitions for women because women regularly still face more challenges in career progression and often react to the prospect of change more cautiously than men. Many of us tend to shy away from a challenge and see difficulties which we fear we will not be able to overcome, and as a result, we may avoid the challenge altogether and accept the status quo. Men, on the other hand, tend to be more open to challenges because they may have developed a sense of self-confidence which many women lack, even those who have made themselves a successful career.

In addition to this, some women who take time out to have children can experience a confidence knock when they return to work and find the readjustment of juggling the demands of life and career challenging. These are, of course, generalisations; and

DOI: 10.4324/9781003353720-1

there are many women with strong self-confidence, just as there are men who lack it.

This book is for those who want to take charge of their career progression and move up to the next level in their career path – whether that may be to team, department, function, or company leader, or simply taking on increased responsibilities within your current role. It is also for those of you who are thinking about a new direction in your working life (such as going it alone) and are trying to decide exactly which direction that should be.

Wherever you're starting from, if you want to move to a position where you have more authority, responsibility, and reach, and where you feel more fulfilled, this book can help. We'll look at some of the unwritten rules about navigating the workplace: working with colleagues, managing your boss, and what to watch out for when you lead a team. We'll also explore the option of moving out of the world of employment and going it on your own – an idea that more and more women are finding attractive.

You can learn to look forward to career moves, rather than be daunted by them. It is never too late to take steps towards having the kind of career and life you want to lead, doing the kind of work that you would like to do, and to be the person you want to be.

In this book, you will find the stories of many women who have made big transitions, and how they overcame obstacles and found fulfilment in the next phase of their life. My hope is that these will inspire you.

THIS BOOK AS YOUR PERSONAL CAREER COACH – START YOUR COACHING JOURNAL NOW

I invite you to soak up the knowledge and insight I share and to adopt what suits you and your situation best. For example, some people will not respond as well as others to vigorous networking, and if you have a naturally cautious temperament, you will be reluctant to engage in this activity. On the other hand, if you don't network, you will miss out on vital information and career opportunities. It is up to you to find what works best for you, but be prepared to move out of your comfort zone in the interests of your career.

During my coaching, I encourage my clients to keep a coaching journal. In the same way, I encourage you to start your career transition journal today. Throughout this book, you will find exercises and suggestions for moments of reflection. These will require time for thought and for actions and sit at the end of the section they relate to as well as being available in the toolkit where you will find them all together so that you can work through them as a toolkit should you wish to use them in this way as well.

As you undertake your journey of career transition, your journal will be the record of your progress. We all spend so much time on our computers, why not choose a beautiful notebook and write your thoughts by hand, perhaps add some doodles or pictures. After all, writing by hand slows us down and allows us to capture the ideas that bubble up from the unconscious that can be so rich and exciting. If writing in a journal is not your preferred medium, consider keeping an audio journal note of recorded dialogue on your phone. This is just as useful. As with much of this book, it is up to you to find what works best for you.

Let's get started!

For your journal

Begin your journal by making a few notes about how you feel at the moment with regard to your job, your career, your life.

Then, think about the following questions and make some brief notes.

1. Why did you pick up this book?
2. How fulfilled are you in your career?
3. What do you hope to change?
4. Is there a time by when you would like this change to have happened?
5. What do you want your working life to look like?

PART I

IDENTIFYING WHAT YOU WANT
AND MAKING IT HAPPEN

WHAT YOU WANT TO DO IS WHO YOU ARE

WORK AS IDENTITY

Work of some kind is vital for our self-esteem, sense of identity, and psychological health. Work gives a meaning and a purpose to our life. We are more likely to attain a sense of fulfilment and happiness (what the psychologist Mihaly Csikszentmihalyi calls *flow*) when we are engaged in a meaningful activity than when we are passively relaxing. Each of us makes our own decisions about how to combine our multiple roles and talents to feel more balanced and fulfilled.

In the course of my work as a career coach with a wide variety of women from all over the world, I have been struck by a clear pattern that has emerged. This is that few of my coaching clients saw their career as a planned journey. In addition, unlike the way that many men tend to compartmentalise their life and career, most of my clients did not see their career as something separate from the rest of their life. This is sometimes driven by the values embedded in their culture, for example the social and political culture in Scandinavian countries enables both men and women to have a more balanced view of life, integrating their career and family in a more holistic way.

A recurring theme in many of the stories I've heard is 'happenstance'. Women used phrases such as 'I never really looked for any of my jobs, they just happened', 'I practically never had an interview', 'I was given the opportunity', 'I never planned my career'

DOI: 10.4324/9781003353720-3

(this from a director!), 'I never had any career goals', and 'I just fell into most of my jobs'. Although this can sometimes work out well (the director had a successful career, rising in the pharmaceutical industry to one of the top jobs in her company), without planning, women all too often end up unfulfilled or in poorly paid and dead-end jobs.

The role that a woman's career plays in her life is rather like one of the themes of a symphony. It enters at a designated point, may even play a dominant role for a while, but then subsides and is heard perhaps as echoes in other parts of the orchestra, or in a different key. In essence, women tend to fit their career around their life, and not vice versa, in a way that men do not. Women go to great lengths to adjust their lives to accommodate others. This attitude can be attributed to both biology and to the way women are socialised from an early age and which is then strengthened and perpetuated by societal structures later in life. The young girl sees how her mother puts the family's needs and wishes first. If she then in turn becomes a mother, she gives herself up to the needs of her child, which is how nature ensures the survival of the next generation. The tension she feels (but does not always admit to) between external expectations and internal aspirations may, however, lead to frustration and resignation, even to depression.

The challenges of serving two masters can be energy-consuming and even debilitating, but they do not have to be. We can learn to make our biological/neurological propensity for adaptation, combination, and emotional sensitivity our greatest advantage. We can manage the inextricably interwoven strands of life and work, and we can learn to be prepared for the challenges that life throws at us and so manage them better.

If you would like to make the theme of your career a more equal, or even dominant one in the symphony of your life, that can be your choice.

I will show you that when you take the time and invest the energy and focus into planning your career moves and becoming more intentional with your decisions, you can greatly increase your chances of ending up in a fulfilling position, and that career moves are less forbidding when you know what to expect and approach them with optimism and self-confidence.

THE IMPORTANCE OF FINDING FULFILMENT AND PURPOSE

Every career move should give you a sense of satisfaction and of meaning in your life which makes you happy to get up in the morning and go to work. Satisfaction, fulfilment, and ultimate success have many definitions, depending on context and individual perspective, and are a combination of our striving to be the best we can be together with a desire to contribute to the world we live in.

We are all pulled in different directions and looking for meaning in our lives which we all find in different places. Moments of fulfilment can be triggered by success (however you define it) when we set our sights on a purpose which we feel is worthwhile. The best way to start your journey towards fulfilment and satisfaction is to start with the simple question: What are my values in life and are these reflected in my work?

KNOWING YOURSELF BETTER = BETTER CAREER CHOICES

UNDERSTANDING YOUR VALUES SYSTEM

Recognising your values helps you gain a clearer picture of who you are and what kind of work you want to do. In addition to fundamental values such as integrity, honesty, equality, freedom, democracy, tolerance, and the right to live your life as you wish, you should consider values that reflect the kind of working environment that would be the best fit for you. Of course, when we choose a type of job, we may be guided by values which later change, and this is okay. The important thing is that you are in touch with what your values are and that you review them regularly to be aware of any shifts in your values that need to be matched to your life choices. Our values are what fundamentally motivate us and so we need to be clear on what they are.

I can think of several coaching clients who started out in the financial services industry with high hopes and in the belief that they valued a top salary and the prestige of working for a headline financial institution, only for these values to pale after a scant few years. In particular, I remember two clients who left that world and chose to work instead in non-profit organisations. They took big salary cuts to work in organisations that embodied what they had come to realise were their new values: serving the community and a good work–life balance. One went to work for an international humanitarian organisation, and the other set up her own small non-profit organisation helping to settle refugees in their

DOI: 10.4324/9781003353720-4

new country. Both have found great satisfaction and have never regretted the move.

There are two kinds of values that will influence your choice of work: those that relate to your attitude around the role of work in your life, and those that relate to how the organisation or company is run, i.e. the working environment, empowerment and independence at work, and an ethical organisational and work culture.

The following exercise for your journal will help you understand what is most important to you and what kind of work or organisation might be the best fit for you.

For your journal

Rank these values according to their importance in regard to your work choices. Note any additional values that are important to you.

Values for the role of work in my life	Not at all important	Important	Very important
Professional status			
Financial gain			
Serving the community			
Stability/security			
Time for family and friends			
Independence			
Adventure			
Gender equity			
Work–life balance			
Recognition			

Now take a look at the second kind of values around how organisations are run.

Values for the working environment	Not at all important	Important	Very important
An ethical culture based on integrity			
Diverse and inclusive			
Non-hierarchical			
Strong team spirit			
Flexible working			
Being in charge of my work and time			
Focused talent development			
A caring and psychologically 'safe' work environment			
Emphasis on innovation and creative thinking			
Strong workforce representation			

Now have a think about these questions.

1. Are you already living and working in a way which honours the things you value?
2. How can you add more of what you value to your work and to your life?
3. What do you need to change in order to fulfil your sense of self?

These are the questions that drive change in our lives. Make a note of your answers to these questions in your journal.

When you are considering a career move, try to discover what values drive the organisation you are planning to join and whether they match your own.

YOUR SUCCESSES SHOW WHAT YOU'RE STRONG IN

Building on from your values, let's reflect on how to take this new-found awareness of your values and use it to delve a bit deeper into understanding your strengths, weaknesses, and work style – all of which will help you then see where you might move next and what would be some good options for you in terms of what you want in terms of a challenge, your lifestyle, the type of work, financially, etc.

It is vital that you know exactly what your strengths are, not only so that you can build on these but perhaps more importantly so that you can then identify how these translate to the workplace and a job or role that would be most suited to you. You can also use these insights to recognise any skills gaps that you need to fill.

To identify your strengths, look first at the moments in your professional life when you have achieved the most – your past success stories. These are the cornerstone to our future successes because they remind us what we excel in and so boost our self-confidence and belief in our ability to go out and do more of the same.

It's also useful to reflect on what comes easily to you – you might not necessarily recognise this as a strength as it feels so natural to you, but think about whether there are any particular skills or types of advice or guidance colleagues, or friends, routinely come to you for?

As you reflect, notice if there are any themes or consistent skills or competencies emerging. How do these feel to you – are they areas of your work or life you particularly enjoy? Are they already reflected in your current role or perhaps something you want to do more of in your professional life?

For your journal

Take several sheets of paper and mark each into two columns, headed as follows:

What I did	My success

I have found that thoughts flow particularly well with pen (or pencil) and paper, but if you prefer to do this exercise on a screen, please feel free to do so. You will have one sheet of paper for each success story that you are going to tell. The exact number is not important, but I would suggest you work with at least five.

Think back over your life and remember some moments when you felt proud of what you had achieved, or someone else acknowledged your achievement or contribution. Choose a mixture from both professional and private life, and semi-professional, e.g. as captain of the swimming team or as organiser of a local community petition. What did you do at university that made you feel proud? What have you accomplished in your professional career so far? What were the highlights? When do you feel most in your comfort zone and confident about what you are doing or contributing?

Take your time to do this exercise. You may want to do it over a few days as you begin to remember your success stories.

What I did: Use as much space as you need. Make some notes about the example. What was the context? Who was involved? What did you set out to do? What did you do? Be sure to include any challenges or problems that you set out to solve.
My success: Why do you consider this story a success story? What did you achieve? Why were you satisfied with your achievement? Did you meet a personal challenge or overcome a previous hurdle? Did other people recognise your success?

Take a moment to feel proud about your successes. It is really important to stop and realise just how much you have already achieved and celebrate this! The stories we tell ourselves about who we are and what we have achieved so far in life are key to self-confidence and knowing what we have to offer.

IDENTIFYING YOUR TRANSFERABLE SKILLS

Now take a look at your success stories again and identify the transferable skills you used in each of your stories, such as being a good communicator, a team player, being creative, and having innovative ideas. We call these 'transferable' because they are valuable in every setting and they are an important factor in the way that we do our work. In addition to proficiency in your own area of expertise, your competence in transferable skills makes you highly valuable for any prospective employer or partner. You need to know which transferable skills you are particularly strong in and also which ones you may need to strengthen. The list of transferable skills in the following exercise includes the most common and sought after, but it is not exhaustive – so feel free to add any that you recognise in yourself, even if they are not in the list.

For your journal

Look back to your success stories and identify which of the following transferable skills you used that contributed to your success in each of your examples (here in 5 success stories).

Transferable skills	1	2	3	4	5
Communication – listening/understanding, negotiating					
Teaching, coaching, mentoring					
Presenting/speaking to a group					
Being innovative					
Planning and organising					
Cultural sensitivity					
Time management					
Diplomacy/tact					
Resilience/perseverance					
Team spirit – bringing people together					
Motivating and inspiring others					
Strategic thinking					
Practical problem-solving					
Decision-making					
Business acumen					

1. Make a note of your top transferable skills.
2. Where are you already using them in your current job?
3. Where could you include them more frequently? Look out for any opportunities to introduce them in your work. For example, if one of your top strengths is negotiating, then see how you could work with clients or with other teams in situations where a negotiating skill is required.
4. Think about a career transition where you could make more use of your top transferable skills. For example, if business acumen, client relations, and strategic thinking are among your top skills, you might like to consider going independent, or at least seeking a professional context where you can make more use of these skills.
5. Which areas do you think you will you need to strengthen for your next career move? How will you do that? Identify ways and opportunities to improve in preparation for your next career move.

WHAT MAKES YOU UNIQUE

When we realise exactly what it is that makes us special and different from all other professionals in our field, we are in a much better position to search for the right fit in our next career move and also much more able to present ourselves to prospective employers or clients in a way that is attractive and matches what they are looking for.

First, you need to know – and be able to talk compellingly about – your professional area of expertise. What are you an expert in? If you were your own advertising agent, what would you say about yourself? What are your specialist areas? Which projects/tasks have you excelled in? What makes you stand out from others in the same field? It is very important to be able to specify exactly what you can do, first to yourself at this stage of self-discovery and awareness, and then later on, when you begin to put yourself out there and talk to other people about what you have to offer.

For your journal

1. Begin with your professional expertise. What is your area of competence (publishing, banking, HR, law, etc.)?
2. Now narrow that down to be more specific about your very particular areas of knowledge – what are you the go-to person for in your firm? What makes you different from all the other accountants or lawyers or project managers?
3. Ask as many people as you like (minimum five) to give you three adjectives that describe you. Ask colleagues, ex-colleagues, managers, coaches, and also friends.
4. Write your professional profile in no more than five lines highlighting your area of expertise and your experience. If you were a can of soup, what would the label say about you?

GETTING TO KNOW YOUR WORK STYLE

What is your work style? It's important to know what your work style is so that you can work out what sort of role you will be best at and where you will be a good fit in an organisation. It is also helpful to be able to bring that awareness to your work to maximise your efficiency.

Are you detail-oriented, practical and good at organising, or creative, someone who sees the bigger picture, open-minded, and always ready to embrace new ideas; or good at seeing how the pieces of the puzzle fit together; do you work best on your own; are you someone who easily creates a rapport with co-workers; are you good at analytical thinking; do you make lists or mind maps? What about work patterns: are you an early or a late bird; do you work slowly but thoroughly, or do you have bursts of energy followed by slumps? Are you good at self-motivating or need more structured management?

It's important to recognise that none of these ways of working is better or worse than another, rather that it's about developing an awareness of how you work. When you know your own work style you can adapt your routine accordingly to ensure you are maximising the quality and efficiency of what you do. It is also immensely helpful to bring this awareness to collaborations and teamwork so that you can complement the way your colleagues deal with tasks.

For your journal

Reflect on the following opposites. Where does your work style fit? Make some notes in your journal.

1. I use lists to prioritise my work/I am flexible about when I do things
2. I like to work things out on my own/I prefer to discuss ideas in a group
3. I complete work quickly/I like to take my time and be thorough
4. I am detail-oriented/I always try to see the big picture
5. I plan everything/I like to leave room for the unexpected to happen
6. I work well under pressure/I don't like stress
7. I am very methodical/I get ideas from everywhere
8. I'm a workaholic/I need downtime to regenerate

WHAT IF YOU'RE NOT ABLE TO MAKE A BIG CHANGE RIGHT NOW?

The previous few sections have focused on developing a deep awareness of your strengths and work style to help you then identify what it is you want to be doing or might be best suited to. That said, it's not always possible for everyone to quickly make the moves or changes they want to. Other responsibilities and restrictions can come in to play which mean any transition will need to be a much more gradual process.

So, what can we do when we are not able to find meaning and fulfilment in our job? Sometimes we find ourselves in a job that is not our ideal choice. If that is true for you, it is worth asking yourself whether you could realistically move. If, for whatever reasons, you decide that is not possible, then I suggest you look for something that you can do to increase your motivation in your current job and make you feel you have a purpose to get up in the morning. For example, you can work towards a diploma or badge, seek out new tasks or responsibilities, train incoming staff, or get involved with mentoring. Using these approaches, you can create for yourself a 'mini' career move within your existing position which will re-motivate you.

You might also consider attending networking events to find out about new and different opportunities and to get some ideas about what else is out there that might give you that satisfaction in the longer term. Becoming more involved and talking to people outside your own immediate circle is in itself invigorating.

Another option is to set yourself the goal of studying a course (Master's, MBA or other professional qualification), which could be useful for a future career move as well as also having the enormous value of stretching you intellectually and facilitating introductions to new people, along with widening your horizon.

Case study

Petra's job as a senior assistant in a consulting firm consisted of preparing complex data sheets for the analysts, organising meetings and preparing budgets. She was competent but the work itself was routine (= boring!) and at the same time the workload was high, so she felt stressed and definitely demotivated. There was nowhere for her to move in the company and her boss was unresponsive to any requests for different assignments. Petra had long wanted to do something more intellectually challenging and interesting, and so she applied to an international MBA course and to her great joy was accepted, with a small scholarship to cover 30% of the fees.

Petra relished the interesting course content, the exchange of ideas between faculty and students, and the camaraderie with her cohort. A new world of fascinating ideas had opened up for her and, although the coursework was quite demanding, she was much happier and more fulfilled than she had been for several years and felt that she was also investing in her professional future.

No matter how stuck you might feel, just a few regular small steps towards a longer-term goal can be just as transformative. If you feel restricted in the changes you can make at present, instead work out how you can best make adjustments in your current role to bring it more in line with your value system, or put plans in place to work closer towards what you want in the longer term.

NAVIGATING CHANGE AND ACQUIRING THE TOOLS TO DO THIS

A POSITIVE (GROWTH) MINDSET TOWARDS CHANGE

Now you have an idea of the kind of working model and environment you would like to find next, it's time to ensure you're in the right mindset to set about making it happen. It's often said that we are what we think and that our thoughts become our reality, so it's vitally important that we get a handle on this and harness our thoughts and inner voice to work with us rather than against us!

Understanding the origins of our own thought processes

Every time we face change, our mind (conscious and unconscious) and body remember similar situations in the past that we or the people we were with went through, either looking forward in joyful anticipation of what lay ahead or worried and fearful. We first learn a pattern for approaching and dealing with change through our family, of course. If your family was basically hopeful and optimistic when facing a change, you will carry this experience over into other groups and situations such as school and university, and into your professional life. But if your early experiences of something new were characterised mainly by doubt

DOI: 10.4324/9781003353720-5

and worry, you will find it harder to feel pleased and excited and will tend to re-create the anxiety you felt in the past.

When we develop our ability for self-reflection and self-awareness, however, we can re-evaluate our experience of the past and recognise that we don't have to react as we did then but can learn to take a more positive attitude to change, especially if, when we look back, things often actually turned out all right. If we take time to reflect, we can see that we do have what it takes to manage the challenge of change and can look forward with confidence to a new adventure.

A positive mindset towards change is a growth mindset, i.e. the belief that you can grow and develop your skills and talents as opposed to a belief that you were born with a fixed set of talents. This mindset has a lot to do with how excited we are to learn. With a growth mindset, we are able to see obstacles and challenges as potentially good things because they offer us opportunities to grow. As professional women, we are constantly tasked with new challenges, confronted with difficult decisions, and asked to think and act strategically for our employers. Transferring this positive mindset to these situations is crucial for your career progression and for planning your next transition strategically, as it will completely shift how you view the challenges and periods of change that you face.

Even if a positive mindset towards change doesn't come naturally to you, you can work at developing it, because one thing is certain: we will all have to go through many career transitions in life, and having the ability to see this as an opportunity to grow and move forward will really help you to shift your relationship with these changes and transitionary periods in your life.

How to cultivate a growth mindset

Imagine you have to prepare answers to three questions about your area of expertise for an internal review and possible promotion. You know there will be stiff competition from two or three co-workers. You submit your answers and have a follow-up conversation with the director who highlights two areas where you did not go into enough detail, and so they inform you that the promotion will go to someone else.

What is your reaction?

The person with a fixed mindset will think: 'Ah, yes, I don't know enough about those areas, I couldn't have done any better. Never mind, that's just how it is.'

The person with a growth mindset will think: 'Right, I'm going to find out about those subjects so that I'm better prepared next time. And, actually, they're interesting and important areas, so I'm going to enjoy learning about those points, too.'

The desire to learn sets the growth mindset apart from the fixed mindset. Our brains have a huge capacity to learn new things if we give them the opportunity, and that means starting out with the premise that even if I can't do it *yet*, I will be able to learn how to do it. If we use a growth mindset every time we push a little out of our comfort zone to learn something new or different, the neurons in our brain can actually form new and stronger connections – we can actually get 'smarter'!

People with fixed mindsets run from a mistake whereas in those with a growth mindset the mistake triggers brain activity – the effort that the brain engages in actually shows up in brain scans; the brain literally lights up!

So, what does this mean if you are considering a career transition and your mindset is still in a 'fixed' zone? It means you are hesitant, lack self-confidence, and don't believe you can do it. But you can move from a fixed mindset to a growth mindset. Here are some simple, but powerful, things you can do.

For your journal

1. Make a note in your journal when you adopt a 'not yet' attitude. Reward yourself for thinking 'not yet… but soon'. You are opening up a path to the future, which is exactly the same as a career transition.

2. Praise yourself more for effort and perseverance rather than just the result. Go back to the 'not yet' mindset!

3. Look at a skill you have improved at some time in your life and recognise that there are things that you have learned. This is especially important if you have a strong fixed mindset and believe you just aren't good at new things.

4. Look back at a time when you failed at something and really identify the reasons why: what can you learn from that analysis? What could you have done differently?

5. Set out to learn something new – anything that you would really like to be able to do or want to know about, and notice your progress, however slow. Practise diligently. After some time (a few weeks or even months), look back at when you started and appreciate your progress. This can work well with a learning buddy so that you motivate and praise each other for the effort you put in.

Case study

After a series of tests and interviews, Rania was not selected for the position in another department that she had coveted. She knew the competition would be strong from internal candidates and she had spent a great deal of time learning about what the department did. After the selection process was complete, the manager told her she was the best candidate on the basis of the written test and presentations but that she had let herself down in the final interview by not paying attention to the type of questions they asked (about her communication, teamwork, and advocacy skills – those transferable strengths!).

Rania and I reviewed her experience together and looked hard at what she could do to improve her interview technique ready for when another position was going to become available in the same department in a few months' time. Adopting a growth mindset meant that Rania felt that there was no way she was not going to be the number one candidate this time! Despite her disappointment, Rania approached the future with a 'not yet... but next time' attitude.

For your journal

1. What patterns of thinking about change have influenced your career journey?

2. Thinking back to change events in your life, how did you handle them at the time? How would you handle them now with more experience?

3. How could you re-frame some of the challenges in your life to make them more exciting and motivating rather than something to be fearful of? Note down some ideas.

VISUALISING YOUR GOALS

A powerful way to prepare yourself for change is to literally see yourself in a different situation – the situation of achievement – and you can do this through visualisation.

Sportswomen prepare for an event both physically and mentally; they train their bodies in their discipline and they also train their minds. One of the mental exercises they do is to imagine themselves in the event, seeing the racing track or ski-slope and visualising every movement right up to the moment of winning. The mind has an extraordinary power to influence our behaviour, and this visualisation helps them to get in the zone and boost their confidence in their ability to win. They are able to see and feel themselves winning.

You can do the same exercise to imagine yourself making a career transition. When I coach, I sometimes say to my client: 'If I were your fairy godmother and could grant your wish for your dream job, what would it be?' I guide them through a visualisation where they see themselves doing the job in as much detail as possible. Visualisation is actually an ancient method not to foresee the future but to influence our approach to it, and it can be applied in all kinds of situations to put us in a positive frame of mind for the task ahead.

Your mind alone will be able to conjure up the different sensations of the experience of the dream job: sight, sound, touch, smell, even taste. When you try it, you will be amazed at the amount of detail you will notice. If you can see yourself doing the job you want, you can find it and fulfil that dream. You can also do this visualisation when you have found a job you think you would like to do, literally to see how it feels to be in the job. This allows you to ask yourself: is this what you want? You could also visualise yourself succeeding at the interview!

Visualisation exercises

Visualisation exercises are a great way of tapping into your unconscious to help you choose your next career move. They work in addition to the practical research you do as they allow you to realise and accept how you feel. You can revisit these exercises in your toolkit.

Exercise 1

1. Find a quiet space and close your eyes. Imagine yourself in the future in a job where you feel fulfilled. Just allow a picture to float to the surface. What do you see? Where are you? What are you doing? Who are the people with you? How do you feel? Afterwards, make a few notes in your journal about what you saw and how you felt.
2. In your visualisation, watch yourself succeeding in the new job. See how you handle the people and the situation you are in.

Exercise 2

1. Create a visual mood board of your aspirations. Ideally, this is an actual board or space on your wall where you can fix sticky notes and pictures, memos, and doodles, whatever comes to hand that you find and that resonates with you while you are thinking about what kind of work you would like to do. Alternatively, you can do this on your computer using a mood board tool such as Pinterest.
2. Don't hold back with the details! The more detail you have in your visual mood board, the closer, more energised, and positive you will feel about achieving that next career move.

REFLECTION

This brings us to the end of Part 1. You have now done the groundwork around understanding yourself better and considering what it is you really want in terms of your next career move or transition. Let's now move on to Part 2 where we will build on this work by starting to explore our options, do the preparatory work towards actually making some changes or transitions, and, finally, learn some skills to underpin this new stage in your career so that you can propel yourself forward with confidence.

Reference

Dweck, Carol S. (2006) *Mindset: The New Psychology of Success*. New York: Random House Publishing Group.

PART II

PREPARING FOR CHANGE

PREPARATION FOR THE TASK

PREPARING FOR CHANGE – UNDERSTANDING YOUR CHOICES

Knowing that you have cultivated a new-found awareness of what you have to offer is important as you get ready to navigate this transitionary phase, and the first step in this process is to ensure you fully understand the implications of your choices and options on all levels – from the practical day-to-day considerations, to how they align with your values and strengths as identified in the earlier sections. Let's look at the main options available to you.

EMPLOYMENT OR SELF-EMPLOYMENT?

When making a decision about how you want your working life to look, you have to make a very fundamental decision about the working model or framework that best suits you and your values. In essence, do you want and need the security and framework of being employed or would the more independent self-employed/entrepreneurial route be the better fit for you? Let's look at both of these in more detail.

Employment with an organisation

Being an employee means you enter into a specific relationship (and contract) with an entity (corporation, organisation, institution, firm) and agree to provide them with your knowledge and

DOI: 10.4324/9781003353720-7

work for which they pay you. There are great benefits to this arrangement for both sides, not least the greater financial security that comes with a guaranteed and regular pay cheque, but as with everything, it can also bring with it some disadvantages.

Whether this is the right fit for you will largely come down to how your ideas and needs around values, money, working culture, and progression fit in with those of the organisation you work for, and how supported and encouraged you feel to progress and develop professionally.

For example, some people very much need to be part of a larger organisation with a set role, regular income, and a clear structure for progression (even if this is limited) as they very much crave a set framework to work within and belong to.

If this resonates with you, then you will be very well placed to pursue your career aspirations and make your transitions within corporate, institutionalised employment structures.

Self-employment or becoming an entrepreneur

In contrast to being employed, if you sense in yourself that you need more self-empowerment, creativity, flexibility, and independence in your working life, you could be well suited to being self-employed.

Women at various stages of life and career are increasingly turning their backs on the corporate and other employer–employee type settings to seek a place for themselves where they can find more personal fulfilment as well as the flexibility to run their own lives around other commitments, such as family, and be their own boss. Sometimes the decision to go it alone comes from necessity, after being made redundant for example. Unemployment due to the Covid-19 crisis triggered a surge in interest in startups and one-person businesses, due to the need for more flexibility in the approach to earning money when whole industries were temporarily shut down.

It is an exciting time to be considering setting up your own business, especially with the myriad opportunities in the tech and digital business fields.

Whether you are a young woman moving straight into setting up your own startup after college or vocational training or are thinking of setting up your own business after however long in an organisational setting, you are in good company. In 2019, there were 4.6 million solo self-employed people in the UK, 1.7 million of whom were women according to a report from IPSE. The number of female freelancers has increased an astonishing 69% since 2008 (ibid.). We are also seeing more women-owned businesses both in the UK and the US. According to a 2020 UENI report, 32.37% of UK businesses are owned by women. The situation is similar in the US, as documented in a 2019 report, with women now owning an impressive 42% of all businesses, which amounts to approximately 13 million firms.

The reasons why women take on the challenge of starting their own business often lie in the lack of opportunities for advancement that many women experience in an organisational culture. And it also has a lot to do with the need and desire to run our own lives, especially if you have children and so are trying to juggle career and motherhood by working part-time or, having taken time out, struggle to regain the career prospects you had before.

While this book does not address the practical side of launching a startup, it does look at many issues that will apply in that setting, such as networking, how to handle people (colleagues, clients, and sponsors), and how to plan your professional strategy and keep track of your progress. The first step, however, is to be realistic about how well suited you are to being self-employed.

If you do decide that the self-employed path is for you, it's worth briefly touching on the characteristics, competencies, and mindset it will be useful for you to adopt. Every freelancer and business owner I have spoken to has underlined that, above all, to start out on the road to being independent you need to know your strengths and weaknesses and be honest with yourself about what you are prepared to do personally. Do not conceal your weaknesses from yourself; if you are a bad organiser or figures are not your forte, you need to ask yourself how big an obstacle this is going to be and what you can do to counter the problem. If you're not going to do the organising, who is? Or are you going to get better at it? (And if not, it's time to bring in some help.) Many things like accounting can be outsourced and so can the day-to-day running of your business if you hire a competent office manager; but you have to ensure you have an overview of your whole business and it must be your hand on the wheel – and you have to be able to pay your accountant and any employees (if you take on staff).

Determination and resilience were also emphasised repeatedly as necessary character traits for an independent business owner. You have to be hard-working and purpose-driven and good at planning, You also have to be good at dealing with problems and setbacks. Look again at your top transferable skills. Do these include planning and organising, time management, resilience/ perseverance, strategic thinking, decision-making, and business acumen?

It is also important to get along with all the people who come into your orbit: associates, co-workers, suppliers, customers, etc. You may have a great business idea and imagine a one-woman setup, but you can't always operate alone; at some stage, you will need support. You will also need people who want your product or service. You need good interpersonal skills to interact in an effective manner with all these people.

Transitioning within your existing field of expertise

A transition to being self-employed in the same field as your previous organisational role obviously has many advantages; for example, a lawyer who worked for a large legal company and then sets up her own law firm has a rich foundation of expertise and experience from which to operate. When I remember my own time managing a classical music ensemble, I recognise now the huge challenge I had set myself by not having the contacts or the background in the classical music world which would have been so helpful. The shift is more straightforward if you stay in the same world where you have the expertise, the background, and the contacts, as Diane in the following case study did.

Case study

Diane had been working in the publishing industry for over 12 years when she took the decision to leave her in-house role to set up on her own. On paper, she had the dream job (a Director level role at a large publishing house) and one she had worked many years to attain, but deep down she felt a pull towards a different way of working and a different lifestyle which was much more in line with her values and life aspirations.

She very much enjoyed her work and her colleagues but longed for more freedom and flexibility – as well as more work–life balance from the long hours and travel she was juggling as an employee.

She took the decision to leave her role and so reached out to her established network of industry contacts for freelance contract work – starting by initially doing some freelance work for the company who previously employed her. She gradually built up a portfolio of clients and was able to create a stable business which still thrives for her seven years later.

Already having built up a reputation within the industry as an employee at a range of different publishing organisations without a doubt aided Diane's transition to self-employment. Having built up her reputation and positive testimonials, she was able to confidently reach out to her network of contacts and past colleagues.

Do you have what it takes to be an independent?

Does the idea of being an independent inspire you and make you feel exhilarated, or is it rather scary to contemplate being out there alone? The answer could be different according to your personal and financial situation. For example, the challenges in pursuing a career when your circumstances are flexible and you have greater independence are very different to the challenges faced by someone with a family, trying to find a way to juggle all their commitments to still fit their values and ambitions. It will also feel different depending on your level of financial commitments and the amount of savings you have in place as a buffer should you need it at any point.

The point is to be aware that there is no right or wrong answer or working scenario here and that you have a choice. It's simply about doing that groundwork to understand which is the best fit for you and your aspirations.

For your journal

1. How attractive does setting up and running your own business appear?
2. How well suited do you believe you are to being your own boss, compared to being an employee?
3. Go back to your success stories and the strengths you recognised you used. Do you have any strengths that you think would help you in a transition to being self-employed?
4. What weaknesses do you have that would be an obstacle to being self-employed and how would you counter them?
5. What experience and expertise do you have that would be helpful?
6. Who do you know in the field you want to set up in that you can talk to?
7. Who do you consider a role model? What can you learn from them?

The following skills and mindset factors are especially useful for being an independent, self-employed woman, whether as a consultant or as a business owner. Check the ones you already have and make a note of those you need to develop.

Skill/Mindset	*Check*	*Develop*
Thinking strategically and planning		
Hard-working		
Resilience and determination		
Organising		
Business acumen and know-how		
Financial know-how and budgeting		
Time management		
People skills		
Decision-making		
Risk management		

WORKING SETUPS

A practical consideration that comes with scoping out how you want your working life to look is to think about the different working setups available and which would best suit you.

The Covid-19 crisis taught us a lot about the way we work – and the way we would like to work. The general consensus was that we had to commute every day from home to work and back again, crushed together with hundreds of others in a bus or train, or stuck in our car in the fumes of a traffic hold-up. Lo and behold we (and our employers) discovered out of necessity that many of us with office-based jobs could do them just as well from our kitchen or bedroom with an improvised arrangement of table and chair. All we needed was a laptop and a stable internet connection.

In a post-pandemic world, employers and employees will work together to devise new, hybrid working setups as solutions for how to work best, and you may have choices on how you want to work. It is important to consider your options here carefully; if you adjusted well to the working-from-home setup, you may be tempted to make that your default working model in future as this will fit in well with your family/carer and other commitments and interests. As long as you are aware that reduced face time with managers could affect your visibility. This may impact your chance to be selected for a project or product, which down the line may affect your career chances – ensure that you take steps to mitigate this risk and you will be able to make the most of a working-from-home arrangement. Make sure to stay closely in touch with your manager and maintain good visibility while staying alert for opportunities in the organisation to bolster your professional value.

For those in the self-employed world who likely already worked at home before the pandemic, take a moment to look into what freelance workspaces are available in your area as this is a great way to maintain a connection to the working world and, more importantly, to network and share ideas with other freelancers/entrepreneurs who may be facing similar challenges – or who simply crave that morning chat at the coffee machine.

There are many models for using these types of workspaces – from very basic, casual weekly drop-in/hot-desking structures to renting a desk or office space for a medium or longer term.

The freelancing and entrepreneur space is very much on the up and with it we're seeing the development of some great communities and working environments, so if working at home full time is not for you, then it is definitely worth investigating this area.

For your journal

1. Do a pros and cons assessment of your workspace arrangements (office/working from home/hybrid).
2. Reflect on what you would like to change.
3. Research accessible freelance workspaces.

MANAGING MONEY

Part of a decision about which path to take is financial. It's the decision around whether you need a regular and secure income or can be comfortable taking a few financial risks; it's also the decision about whether fulfilment for you means pursuing a goal of earning a high income or could mean taking a pay cut (if only initially in some cases). Either way, this decision needs to be in line with your wider values – and needs – around earning. Only you will know what your financial obligations are and what the minimum is you want to earn – as well as what potentially higher target you have in mind. There's no right or wrong here, but it's vital to have this clear in your mind and fully understand what comes with each earning scenario before you make any moves.

If you leave your corporate cocoon to set up on your own, it's important to ask yourself some questions. At what stage will you be able to match the salary you were earning previously – if that is what you aspire to – and how will you finance your life until then? Do you have savings in place if needed? Will you manage your tax obligations yourself or hire an accountant? Will you take a monthly salary? Which business bank account will you go with? What will the setup and running costs of your business be? All these things need to be considered *before* you take the leap into self-employment.

While it's most definitely not just about the money, decisions do need to be made with a very clear and honest appraisal of your finances.

For your journal

1. Do a realistic assessment of your finances – get help if you need it.
2. If you are considering becoming independent, research funding.
3. Research the typical fee/pay structures for freelance/self-employed professionals in your industry.
4. Find an accountant if you think you need one.

5

EXPLORING NEW PATHWAYS AND OPPORTUNITIES

In this next section, we will build on the work already done around understanding your values and shifting into a positive, growth mindset and move forward to facilitate that process of understanding what options you have and how to go about turning them into real opportunities.

You will make many career moves throughout your life, beginning with the transition from school, college, or higher education to the workplace. It is liberating to realise that, wherever you are in your life and career, there is a wealth of opportunities out there, and for that very reason, it is also important to remain open-minded about what kind of job you want.

WHERE ARE THE OPPORTUNITIES?

Start with your interests and passions. What fascinates you? What drives you? What are you good at? Then dig down to find out what sort of workplaces exist that match your interest and profile, and what kind of jobs people do there. Until you know something is out there, you can't know whether you might want it, or whether you would be able to do it.

Tap into all the different sources of information at your disposal to find out as much as you can about potential places that could interest you: careers services and platforms, LinkedIn, other social media platforms, recruiters, friends and family, and friends of friends. Talk to people you meet and find out what they do. Talk to representatives from different companies and organisations.

DOI: 10.4324/9781003353720-8

The more diverse your sources of information, the more ideas you will get for all kinds of exciting potential jobs that grab your attention, and you will begin to see a range of jobs or organisations you might like to work with.

CREATING YOUR OWN OPPORTUNITY

Sometimes you can even invent a job and then create an opportunity or role around this. This is exactly what many entrepreneurial women are doing with start-ups – recognising a consumer need and turning it into a market opportunity by creating a product or a service to fill that need.

Many start-up examples are found in the tech industry, which is continually enabling us to create new and exciting solutions to problems. The start-up Nourish3d and Script3d, founded by the young female entrepreneur Melissa Snover, is a great example of this. It pioneers personalised health solutions across nutrition and medicine through products such as vegan vitamin sweets created using visionary food technology and 3D printing.

Female tech entrepreneurs are everywhere. Look at the many apps that make our lives easier and at the online solutions that businesses need, such as Appointedd, an online booking and scheduling system that works in all time zones from any device, founded by another young female entrepreneur, Leah Hutcheon, which has some impressive clients.

The point is to find something that you are passionate about that matches your values, interests, and expertise. It's also about being open to researching and discovering more about where the opportunities around this type of work lie – even if this ultimately results in carving a role and company out for yourself. Just because it's not been done yet, doesn't mean it's not a great opportunity or the right one for you. Do your research, reach out to the wider community and see where you end up!

Let's take a look at what happened to Jessica, who, after several jobs – some more satisfying than others – systematically searched for one that would suit her needs, passion, and professional expertise.

Case study

Jessica had studied biology and zoology at university and had obtained a BSc in Natural Sciences. Her passions were nature and animals; she loved being outdoors. After university, she did a couple of internships, one as a researcher for an NGO, working in a small community in Vanuatu, and another working on a nature documentary for the BBC, and she acquired good research and communications skills. She then took a job in a government department dedicated to bringing environmental issues into education. Although she owned the subject, Jessica was unhappy in a bureaucratic working environment. She considered going back to documentary films again, where she had enjoyed the work itself, but, now in her early thirties, she realised she wanted more stability and a better salary than that would offer her.

She started by researching potential areas of employment on the internet, and then targeted contacts through her family, her university alumni group, and LinkedIn, and met with them to find out about their jobs. She identified the types of employment that attracted her most and where she believed she might find a fulfilling job: environmental consultancies; national and international organisations with an environmental agenda; and government environmental departments. I asked Jessica to write her own dream job description and we also did a visualisation, which she found to be a very powerful exercise. Her next step was to make a list of actual employers for all three potential employment contexts and then to talk to someone inside those organisations to gather specific information about them and what they were looking for. This was vital, because Jessica at first believed an additional academic qualification such as a Master's or even a PhD would be necessary, which proved not to be the case.

All this research took time, but it was time well spent. Jessica spent about four months gathering her information before she started applying for positions. Because she had done such detailed research she was well informed about what potential employers were looking for and how she could position herself. After interviews with three prospective employers – two consultancies and one foundation – Jessica received two offers and accepted a position with a well-respected sustainability consultancy. She later told me that when she compared the offer with the dream job description she had written a few months earlier, they were very similar.

For your journal

What are you really interested in doing? Now is the time to lay the groundwork for including more of what really interests you in your work.

1. Brainstorm or doodle everything that interests you including not only work-related activities but also things that currently have nothing to do with your work.
2. Separate out the things that are strictly personal, such as your family.
3. Now look again and identify the activities that you would like to do more of in your next career move. Allow yourself to think outside of the box – be brave! These could include:

   a. Areas that you could include in your current work context but perhaps in a different role, such as taking on a managerial role, working more with clients, negotiating, etc.
   b. New activities or areas that are different from what you do currently but that you would like to explore.
   c. Different contexts, such as working independently, but still doing the kind of work you do currently.

4. Identify what really interests you – what would you be excited to do next?

PROFESSIONAL QUALIFICATIONS AS A CURRENCY FOR PROGRESSION

In the course of your information-gathering, you may come to realise that an additional qualification would be useful in order to get a job in a potential area of employment, but you should always check if this true before committing to any programme of study. As we saw in the case study above, Jessica believed at first that a Master's in Environmental Sciences would be an asset for her applications to environmental organisations but when she researched jobs, she found it was not actually a requirement.

It will depend on the industry and on the individual organisation as to what qualifications are required. If you are passionate about your subject and want to learn more and go back to university to do a Master's in the same subject as your Bachelor's degree, because you love it, that is absolutely your decision (as long as you can finance it!). However, do not be fooled into thinking that the Master's initials after your name will inevitably make you a more eligible candidate than if you only hold a Bachelor's degree. This is not always the case and could well mean that all you are doing is postponing the work of looking for a job, which means that when you do launch yourself onto the job market, you will be competing with younger graduates and will have no experience to offer that will make you stand out from the crowd.

In most cases, a Bachelor's degree plus some years of experience in the right field is as or even more useful than a Master's. The same applies to those of you with a Master's considering doing a PhD, which is usually only a requirement for academic posts. That said, professional diplomas are also valued in many fields just as much and sometimes even more than academic qualifications, and employers always look for specific, industry-relevant qualifications.

In addition to your main qualification, it is often a good idea to get an additional professional qualification, certificate, or badge to complement your existing qualifications. For example, in areas such as project management, leadership skills, or IT. Alternatively, you can attend courses in a specialised area of your own field and receive a certificate of attendance. Continuous professional development (CPD) is not only a tick-the-box activity; it's a really important way of staying current with developments in the workplace throughout your career and for positioning yourself for your career moves.

When you are looking to make a career move or return to work after a gap you must check that you are up to date with your know-how and any developments in your field. Get the most current information by using your network, attending conferences and industry events. If you discover gaps in your qualifications, knowledge, or skills, you can fill these by attending courses, many of which are online through professional digital course companies, and you can obtain a badge or a certificate to prove what you have learned.

When choosing a course, it is a good idea to make sure that the institution is accredited or recognised (if needed) and that the credentials you receive are recognised by the companies in your field.

If you have qualifications from a country different to the one in which you are now living and working, you must have your foreign qualifications approved by the relevant authorities. Do not be tempted to take a job that is far below your qualifications, or if you do, then do so with your eyes wide open. This is a trap that many women fall into, in the belief that any job is better than no job. This depends on your circumstances, and if you need the job desperately, then learn all you can at that job and be on the lookout to move. It can be quite hard to move up a couple of levels in a role, so if you can hang on until you find a suitable job at your level then do, otherwise you may find yourself stuck. In some settings, notably institutions belonging to the public sector including the civil service and international organisations such as the humanitarian organisation, it is difficult to move from one category of staff to another; so, I recommend that you only apply for professional positions and not be tempted to accept an administrative post.

For your journal

1. Are my qualifications valid and current? Do I need additional qualifications?
2. Am I aware of the main professional course providers?
3. What are the latest developments in my field that I should know about?
4. Am I up to speed with my complementary skills, such as IT?
5. What do I need to do to bring my skills portfolio up to date?

6. What special expertise or experience can I offer an employer?
7. Consider any challenges you may face and how you expect to counter them.

TESTING THE WATER

Sometimes it is possible to test out a new field before making a move. Temporary appointments, maternity or paternity replacements, consultancies, and internships are all ways of testing the water. Firms benefit from the opportunity to test applicants in real-time rather than in an expensive on-boarding and probationary period which may incur the costs of re-recruiting, and applicants themselves get to test whether the role and organisation is right for them too.

Internships are a great way of starting out in a new industry, though they can sometimes disappoint when the experience may not turn out to be what you expected and at the end of the six-month internship period, you are out on your own again. That said, an internship in a field in which you are interested is potentially better than working in a bar while you are deciding where to move – although possibly not as good for your bank balance. Unfortunately, a key element of many internships is that they are either unpaid or pay only expenses, which means that not everyone is in a financial situation to be able to do them. This is changing, and many companies now recognise the value of the internship with a stipend. An internship can be a stepping-stone to a job you love if you use the time to make good connections, gather information, and gain experience in the field. The case study below highlights where internships can be a great way to work out exactly what it is you want to do and make connections.

There is not always a clear or obvious path when it comes to finding exactly what it is you want to do, but by being open and exploring different avenues and maximising the opportunities for learning as you look at each one, you will soon gain insights about what you want to be doing and then be able to focus your energy on moving confidently towards that goal.

Case study

Charlotte graduated with a BA in International Relations. Having little idea what to do next, she opted first to do a Master's in International Law, a logical additional string to her bow. Although she completed the course, she came to the conclusion that she did not want to work in international law, so it was back to the drawing board. Through a family connection, she was able to get a six-month internship in a national central bank, which she found interesting, but not sufficiently enough to induce her to go into banking. After several applications, she started in a position at a PR company in London with a large financial services client base, where the work seemed to bridge her qualifications and interests very well. During the probationary period, however, Charlotte realised she did not want to stay in financial services and looked around for something to match her interests better.

Charlotte had been interested in wine for some time and after completing a sommelier course for fun, decided she would love to work in the wine industry. She was able to pull together all her qualifications and experience – including her internship time – to apply for a PR position advertised with a wine broker in the City of London that had many international corporate and private clients. Impressed by her international outlook, her PR skills, and her financial services experience, they offered her instead of the PR job a wine marketing position with full training and they paid for her to complete a professional wine diploma. A great career transition success story which drew on her earlier internship long after she had completed it!

6

THINKING CREATIVELY ABOUT YOUR NEXT CAREER TRANSITION

'What do I want to do with the rest of my life?' is a question many women ask themselves at some point. Perhaps work has become routine and not as fulfilling as it used to be; you begin to feel disenchanted and are no longer sure you are where you want to be. This sometimes happens when a company does a re-structure or after a takeover when your position as you knew it no longer exists. Or it could be when a disruptive personal event such as a divorce causes you to re-think your life, or when your children leave the home, or after an illness or a death. You begin to look around for new channels for your energy and accumulated knowledge outside the strictures of organisational work.

Some women opt out of their previous professional context and re-invent their life to do something completely new based on long-held dreams, turning their passion and talent into a brand-new venture. For some, financial rewards no longer play such an important role compared to other values and they seek to put purpose into their lives.

If thoughts of trying something *really* new are buzzing around in your head, you can take inspiration from the following stories of women who took their careers and lives into their own hands and dared to do something different. This could be freeing yourself from an organisational set-up and branching out on your own in your known profession or it might mean trying something completely different.

DOI: 10.4324/9781003353720-9

Thinking creatively about your next career transition means listening to your hopes and dreams and then taking the plunge. It means daring to have the adventure that you want. It is never too late.

For your journal

1. Reflect on the work you did in Part 1 of this book around your values and aspirations. What does this insight tell you about you as a person and what your ideal work might be?
2. Reflect on your dreams and wishes.
3. What would you like to do with the rest of your life?
4. Write a story about yourself in this new life.
5. Draw or find a picture that portrays for you your new career and hang it on your wall.

DOING SOMETHING DIFFERENT WITHIN YOUR CURRENT SECTOR

After reflecting on what you want, it may be that you discover that you're not actually that far from achieving it and that your transition is more of a subtle shift to doing something slightly different within the sector you already work in. Simply changing specialism, department, or function (working internally or as a consultant) could give you the career and life reboot you're looking for.

Our case study below shows a great example of someone who re-invented themselves to work as an independent consultant for the same organisation where she started her career (albeit in a different role). Her experience of working within the organisation in a different capacity gave her the insight and understanding of its challenges and made her an invaluable and much sought-after business partner.

Case study

Julia's story is full of exciting new ideas and challenges, constant change, and growth from one career phase to the next. Having first trained and worked as a midwife within the NHS, after various internal restructures she recognised she yearned to have a larger operational role. She retrained to acquire a professional qualification in Organisational Development, which she put to good use as co-lead of a Leadership Development Academy within the NHS.

After a while, however, she discovered that the goals they were supposed to pursue were not aligned with her values and she had a distinct feeling of being a square peg in a round hole. She took the drastic step of resigning from her job with no safety net. She looks quite cheerful as she remembers that time because, she says: 'I knew I could reinvent myself.' She had utter faith in her ability to take on a new challenge, all the while remaining true to herself. She is fearless in her appetite for a new challenge, curious as to what could emerge, happy to go out into the unknown. And indeed, within a week, she had been invited as an independent consultant to help a team in the NHS with the organisational challenges they were struggling with.

Through word-of-mouth, she was regularly passed on to new teams who needed her help. Her latest transition was to become an associate of a training company that works with theatre and coaching to support teams in their organisational development and sustainable performance.

Along her career path, Julia has acquired many qualifications, including several coaching diplomas, a Master's in Medical Anthropology, a certificate in Organisational Development, and she is working towards another Master's degree in Transformational Coaching.

Julia's story is a great illustration of how being in touch with yourself and your values, combined with creativity and adaptability, can carry you forward and open many new doors. She is always on the lookout for her next career transition opportunity.

MAKING A BUSINESS OUT OF A HOBBY

Sometimes businesses grow from something that was originally a hobby or a passion such as a travel blog, an interest in fitness and health, or a passion for making your own cosmetics, as in Marcia's case below.

Case study

Marcia had been an executive secretary practically all her professional life. For 15 years, she had worked as personal assistant to the HR manager of a large international company in London. She was divorced, with no children. She fully enjoyed the international flair of London, the city where she had lived and worked for nearly 20 years, although she originally came from a small town in Croatia. She had attained a top job, with an excellent salary. Yet, there was something missing. Her work was largely repetitive, and she no longer felt any excitement or even interest in what was going on in the company. Professionally, she had reached a plateau, where her job seemed routine and dull. About this time, she broke up with her partner of many years. Marcia had saved up some money and so decided to fulfil a long-standing dream: to take some time out and see the world.

When she returned to 'real life' after a year, Marcia had already thought about what she wanted to do with the rest of her life. She had a hobby: she enjoyed making beauty creams and cosmetics, which she did in her kitchen, wrapping them beautifully and giving them as birthday and Christmas presents to her friends and family. When she was in her 'lab', she felt a great glow of happiness and a sense of achievement, and all the recipients of her beauty products assured her that they were very special. The germ of an idea began to grow.

Marcia signed up for an evening course on starting your own business and loved it. Her administrative experience stood her in good stead, and she quickly mastered the concepts of creating a business plan, doing market research, and learning basic marketing skills. She used her network to gain information from people who had started their own business, she talked to her bank manager about a loan, and, finally, she founded her own company which makes environmentally sustainable cosmetic products with ingredients not tested on animals, marketing them online. She has never worked harder, but she finishes work every day with a huge sense of accomplishment.

Marcia had no idea whether she could be a businessperson when she set up her own business, but she knew she was very good at administration and paperwork, budgets, planning, and organising. In short, she knew a lot about the components of running a business, even if she had never done so before. She outsourced tasks to professionals so that she could concentrate on the areas where she felt comfortable.

After three years, Marcia realised with great pride that she had made the professional transition from department head PA to business owner very successfully.

Marcia's experience reminds us to recognise what we want out of our professional lives and to find a way to make it happen.

BIGGER AND BETTER – WITH A BUSINESS PARTNER

Some one-woman businesses stay at just that; you may discover that being a consultant or freelancer on your own with a support network of professionals and perhaps also associates is your ideal working arrangement and gives you the professional and financial rewards you are looking for. But sometimes businesses grow beyond something that can be managed by an individual and a decision needs to be made about how to move forward. This case study shows the example of Juliette, whose one–woman business grew exponentially and reached a tipping point at which she needed to bring in extra help to support that growth.

Case study

Juliette was a catering officer in the RAF but left after a restructure to set up on her own, doing business lunches and small receptions once a week. Over time, she built up a reputation by word-of-mouth and her venture grew into an extremely successful business, catering business lunches and up to four weddings a week.

The catering industry is fast-paced, physically demanding, and highly competitive and Juliette realised that in order to keep up she needed a partner. Her friend Nancy came in as a business partner quite early on and in addition, they also employ a few fixed staff supplemented by as many temporary kitchen and wait staff as are needed for the events they supply.

Juliette attributes her success to determination, hard work, and a very down-to-earth, no-nonsense attitude. She discovered she had a great talent for business but is also quick to say she had wonderful support in Nancy, as they complemented each other's skills and talents. Juliette was the business head and the external relations manager; she knew where she wanted to position the business and worked hard at making that vision come true and expanding her client base.

Nancy was great at interpersonal relations with the kitchen and wait staff and together they made a great team. Juliette relied on external associates for specialist tasks such as tax, accounting, website, and legal work contracts.

This was a very different operation than where Juliette started, catering one or two business lunches a week. She underlined the amount of hard work that running her business entailed: 'In the hospitality industry you're always working when everyone else is having fun; you work evenings, you work weekends. I hardly saw my children when they were teenagers, but I had to work to pay my bills [Juliette was widowed quite young], but, yes, I love the buzz. It's rewarding to successfully pull it off.'

TECH STARTUPS

It is very exciting to see the number of women entrepreneurs who have introduced innovations to many different industries with apps for customers, technological solutions for businesses, and amazing new products.

Let's take two examples: Julie Grieve founded her business Criton in 2016 to solve the problems hotels face by offering their guests a fully digital guest experience from booking to checkout. Her practical tech solutions to these problems have transformed the way small hoteliers can simplify their operations. Julie studied Business Studies and Tourism and Leadership and worked in the luxury services apartment sector for several years. So, when it came to setting up her own business, she had a good theoretical foundation, practical experience in the tourism industry, and a keen eye for the problems that the industry needed to solve. Her strengths are business sense and negotiating skills and also a genuine desire to help people, evidenced by her volunteer and mentor work. But first and foremost, she has a clear vision for her business: to offer tech solutions to a strong, well-functioning tourist industry to help them serve the needs of their guests as smoothly as possible.

A clear vision is something that Melissa Snover shares. In all the businesses Melissa has either been director of or founded, she has combined her business and entrepreneurial know-how with a strong sense of mission. Melissa also has a business and financial background, and her vision is to provide delicious and healthy snacks and 'sweets' for busy people. Nourish3d and Script3d use cutting-edge 3D printing technology to make customised vitamin sweets. On her website, she gives a mini tutorial on developing a business from the conception of an idea to market research and funding, and through to the launch. What comes through very clearly is her resolve, determination, and perseverance, strengths we meet time and time again in women who run their own business.

TEACHING

After busy corporate careers, many people are turning their knowledge to teaching, with the aim of doing something meaningful – helping light a spark in young people's minds and also experience a sense of reward themselves by doing so. Organisations such as *Now Teach* recruit people who have had successful careers in various professions into teaching and support them in that move. It is a deceptively simple and brilliant idea, because people who are tired or frustrated and demotivated in the career they have had for many years are attracted by the new challenge of teaching but need help to put the transition into practice. They are often driven by a desire to do good by today's children and bridge the gap between education and the 'real world', which is so often lacking in schools. *Now Teach* acts as a support system, providing information and guidance, access to teacher training opportunities, and, perhaps most importantly, a social network in the cohort of people who are in the same boat.

Rachael Kaykobad of *Now Teach* emphasises two things to be successful in a new environment: good preparation in order to fully understand what the new career is about, coupled with an appetite to learn. This learning mindset will carry on throughout the transition and beyond and is one of the main messages of this book: you have to be prepared to keep on learning all the time.

Tamara's story is a shining example of the learning mindset and an inspiration for all those thinking about teaching.

Case study

After a degree in Animation, Tamara started her working life in TV film production (she laughs when she says what she really did was make tea!) but left fairly soon to set up her own small business together with two people experienced in the industry, making corporate films for businesses and charities, which she did for over 20 years. Her business partners were somewhat older than her and when they came to retirement age, she was faced with the decision of what she should do next. She had shared a particularly strong professional relationship and the same work ethos with both her business partners and feared that could never be replicated with other partners. She also asked herself the question: 'Do I want to keep doing this for the next 15–20 years?' The answer was a clear no. She had been thinking for some time about changing her professional life completely to do something new, sustainable, exciting, inspiring, and fulfilling; teaching at primary school level was the idea that had been buzzing in her head which she felt would fulfil all those criteria. After talks with teachers at her daughter's school, where they had a strong training focus, and with her husband and two daughters, she made the decision to go ahead with the training through School Direct. She was adamant that this was not an experiment; she wanted to make the best choice for her new career in the full realisation that this was going to be intense – life-changing, in fact.

Tamara's career transition couldn't have happened at a more challenging time; she started her intensive training in 2019 and was two weeks into her placement when lockdown was imposed, making school life unbelievably difficult – Tamara used the word 'eventful'! It was learning on the go, but Tamara says she was well supported by her colleagues and the learning team.

For Tamara, the move to teaching has been challenging but exciting and overwhelmingly satisfying: 'I wouldn't change it for the world, I wish I'd done it earlier', she says. She is fascinated by her new environment, of course, and loves playing a fundamental part in the way the children learn.

She found that being optimistic, determined and persevering, and having a bedrock of positivity were all things that helped her through her career transition. She also emphasises that 'it feels fantastic to be learning; it's invigorating and rejuvenating', the mindset towards learning that we find at the core of all successful transitions. Tamara likes to say she moved from a position of conscious incompetence to unconscious competence.

Tamara also underlined how life-changing her new career was for her family and how her husband stepped up to taking on much of the domestic role that she had previously fulfilled. Support from her whole (extended) family was also key to her success.

You may have a gift for teaching that you can use even if you do not have a teaching qualification or want to go through the arduous process of acquiring one. Consider teaching English as a foreign language: literally millions of people all over the world, from children to university students to adults, want to learn (better) English. TEFL is one of the best-known qualification providers, and they will train you. A TEFL qualification might just be the passport to getting to know a new part of the world. It is not only within for-profit schools that teachers are required; thousands of refugees are struggling to learn the language of their new country. Programmes run by local governments and NGOs like Refugee Action all need volunteers to support refugees to gain self-confidence and improve their English.

Or consider signing up with one of the tutoring companies that offer a service matching tutors with students where tutors work on a self-employed basis, which means the company acts in principle as an online matching agency. You register as a tutor online, stating your experience, your location, and your fee; from there, prospective clients find you via the website. Both children and adult learners use tutoring services. One of the advantages is that you can tutor partly or exclusively online, using one of the online platforms.

CREATIVE DISCIPLINES

Frustrated or disappointed with their career or simply plateaued with a feeling of nowhere left to go, some women on the lookout for a career change revive a talent for writing, painting, drawing, or something else creative which has been dormant and which they then allow to flourish; a new career path has been discovered. You can let your imagination run freely and use those inventive ideas which very often lead to great fulfilment. This may not be hugely financially lucrative, but this leads us back to our values – what is really important for you at this stage of your career and life?

Let's look at just one example of an imaginative idea in the story of Shila.

Case study

Shila had had a good career as a HR manager in a multi-national retail company but there came a time when she realised that she had been under great stress which had actually caused her to fall ill frequently, and she also realised that she no longer really enjoyed her job. She resolved to find something less stressful and more interesting; something different. Shila had long been fascinated by her family history. When Shila was three, her family came to the UK from Sri Lanka where her mother had worked in the tea plantations and her father had run a small shop. Her parents set up their own business, starting with one convenience store and subsequently expanding to three stores. Shila had family photographs, letters, and documents spanning nearly 80 years, and she set about learning more about Ceylon, the country where she was born.

Shila discovered a course at a city university on writing one's autobiography; she loved the course and over a few months she wrote her family's story. When she realised that there were many people who would love to do the same thing, she trained with the course providers and subsequently set up her own online business in which she conducts webinars to teach people how to write their autobiographies. Skilled at working with people in a training context from her HR background, Shila was able to convey her passion for each project and teach the skills needed for autobiographical writing. She is a much sought-after tutor and although the pay is not high, she feels rewarded by the thanks she receives and is very fulfilled. She is no longer under great stress and looks forward to every day.

Whatever your creative idea is, you can make it work for you if you are passionate and determined. Remember as well that 'creative' can be interpreted in many ways in order to turn your passion into your next career. Do you have a talent and a love for dressmaking that you would love to turn into a business of your own? The runaway success of the TV series *The Great British Sewing Bee* has triggered much interest and many of its contestants have launched independent ventures.

Networking and support apply here as well; going it alone in any discipline does not mean doing everything alone.

For your journal

1. Write down what you truly love doing (your favourite hobby or pastime) and reflect on whether you are good enough at it to turn it into a business and whether you would want to (sometimes a hobby is something to be enjoyed in your private time!).
2. Who would pay you for your product or service?
3. Research similar offerings online. Find out what they charge and how their business is structured.

OR

1. Write down what idea you have to do something entirely new even though you have no prior experience.
2. Research who needs this.
3. Research how to learn this using your network.

Being creative about a potential change in direction for your career often means tapping into a desire or idea that has been slumbering in your unconscious or your memory for a while. Tamara, who moved into teaching when she was nearly 50 years old after a career in business film production, admits that the idea had been germinating for a long time. She had enjoyed watching her daughters learn at primary school and had been impressed with the way they were taught; the process of how children learn had fascinated her from that time on, but it was not until many years later that the idea came to her as a career option, triggered by the external factor of her business partners retiring. It is never too late to turn to something new that appeals to you for fundamental reasons. You just need courage, determination, and, of course, the right support.

REFLECTION

We have now come to the end of Part 2 which has equipped you with the information and insight to review your options and identify which scenario or working setup might be best suited for you and what you want out of your next move. I hope that this part of the book has also opened your mind to the opportunities around you and encouraged you to start thinking more creatively about the direction you might choose to go next and how to start investigating further and making things happen.

Now that we have looked at understanding who you are, what you want, and how to seek out new opportunities, we're ready to move on to Part 3 where we shift our focus to taking these ideas and ambitions and transforming them into concrete opportunities. We will also look at the key skills you need to cultivate in order to do this so that by the end of Part 3 you will have a toolbox of skills to propel yourself forward in your career – in whichever direction and path you now know you want to travel on.

PART III

GETTING TO WHERE YOU WANT TO GO AND CULTIVATING THE SKILLS THAT UNDERPIN SUCCESSFUL CAREER TRANSITIONS

7

TRANSFORMING IDEAS AND WISHES INTO CONCRETE OPPORTUNITIES

RESEARCHING OPTIONS AND MAKING IT HAPPEN

Transforming your wishes and ideas for change into concrete options is the key step after carrying out your research into what opportunities are out there. You do this by identifying your 'columns of opportunity' (see the Five O'Clock Club book series on the career search process for this and other useful exercises), starting with your wish-list and the ideas you have for the type or area of work you want. This will help you to systematically research and find specific employers that you would be interested in working for – or indeed just to establish who's out there and actively employing in your chosen area.

> ### Case study
>
> Andrea was a marketing/branding expert who had progressed through various industries, from entertainment to retail (baby foods, a multi-branch clothing and interior design store) and finally to property development, steadily climbing the career ladder successfully.
>
> Lately, she had taken some time out to reconnect with her family when her sister was diagnosed with cancer. Contemplating going back to work, Andrea realised that though she definitely wanted to stay in marketing, she thought she would like to work in a more project-management context. She was considering the healthcare industry, having witnessed her sister's struggle with healthcare options, and decided she would prefer to work in an SME (small or medium-sized enterprise).
>
> Andrea drew up her wish-list to include all the points detailed in the columns below, along with the geographical location of where she

DOI: 10.4324/9781003353720-11

Wish-list	COLUMN 1 Healthcare institutions, private hospitals	COLUMN 2 Alternative medicine companies	COLUMN 3 Pharmaceutical companies	COLUMN 4 Sports facilities, gyms	COLUMN 5 Care facilities
Marketing Project management Healthcare Medium-sized organ- isation Location in or near Bristol					

wanted to be. After much thought, she decided on five areas where she potentially saw herself. These were her columns of opportunity.

After some thought, Andrea added a sixth column: her own marketing or branding consultancy. Her next task was to fill the columns of opportunity with names of potential employers in the region where she wanted to work.

One of Andrea's biggest challenges was how to present herself as a credible candidate for a job in the healthcare industry without any prior experience in that area. She felt it would not be enough to simply rely on her marketing credentials and wanted to be well prepared. She planned to gather information about the industry and identify where marketing skills were being used in a project framework, and at the same time become visible to key people.

Andrea mined her personal and social networks for contacts in the healthcare industry and attended conferences and events (including online) where some of the heavyweights of the industry were present. As often at this kind of event, the really interesting things happen on the side-lines, not in the official programme of talks and presentations. With this in mind, Andrea's goal at these events was to meet or get some leads on some of the decision-makers in companies and institutions that could be potential employers and organise a one-on-one meeting with them at a later date. She did her research on the industry and so, when she met key stakeholders, she was able to explain convincingly where she believed she would fit in as a marketing expert.

Eventually, Andrea narrowed her columns down to two: healthcare institutions (hospitals and clinics) and care facilities. She had a list of 16 potential places of employment, which she put in order of interest. She used her network (which was now full of people in the healthcare industry!) to get face-to-face meetings with people in healthcare facilities. These meetings gave her a chance to get more information about each organisation and she was also able to practise making her pitch as a marketing project manager without actually being part of the recruitment process.

In fact, one of the people she talked to was so impressed that his clinic offered her a job to manage a marketing project for a new specialist facility they were about to open.

Andrea was convincing in her 'pitch' because she knew what her strengths were and, because she had already done her research about the industry, she knew what they needed in marketing. She was able to make the link between their needs and what she could supply. This is always the key to any conversation about a job, whether it's a formal interview or not.

Meet Andrea, who is seeking the right next career move. We will follow her in how she decided which career options to target.

If reaching out to people seems daunting to you, start with people in your network who you know will be receptive – there may be some surprises there. For example, alumni from your university, whom you don't know, will usually be very happy to help you with information.

For your journal

The columns of opportunity table is a structured way of collecting your ideas about where you would like to work: the kind of work you want to do, the type, size, and location of the organisation you would like to work in, and any special thoughts you have.

1. Create your own columns of opportunity – 4–6 columns are a good number.

Opportunities		1	2	3	4
My area of expertise					
My wished focus, e.g. small projects					
My target context					
My desired type of employment					
My desired location					
Additional thoughts					

Your columns are not set in stone – you can add or take away at any time as your research progresses. The main thing is to proactively and methodically do your research into what is available that matches your profile and interests.

Andrea's expertise was in marketing, but she wanted to move into the context of healthcare. These are her columns of opportunity.

Opportunities		1	2	3	4
My area of expertise	Marketing/ branding	Healthcare institutions/ private hospitals	Alternative medicine companies	Pharmaceutical companies	Gyms/physio institutes
My wished focus	Small projects				
My target context	Healthcare				
My desired type of employment	Small/ medium– sized (SME)				
My desired location	Bristol/West country				
Additional thoughts	Must match my values				

2. The next step is to research potential employers that match the criteria with all the resources available to you, on the internet, through your network, in industry associations, forums, etc., and insert the names of these organisations and companies into your table.

3. Methodically research these potential places of employment and find out as much as you can about them. Reach out to talk to people at these organisations to get more information.

4. As you do your research, you will begin to see a clear picture of which companies you would like to work for and what you could offer them. You will also realise where you do **not** want to work – which is also valuable!

GETTING A FOOT IN THE DOOR

Your next task is to find a way into these companies to introduce yourself and gather information about the company and the kind of skills and expertise they need. Ideally, this would be through a team lead or department head. HR managers are not always your best contact, because they do not usually make hiring decisions or have full knowledge of the day-to-day requirements of specific roles or departments. That being said, if you have an HR manager in your network, then by all means reach out to them to find out what is going on in their company and/or industry and ask for their help in connecting you with a mid- or senior-level decision-maker.

Leads for contacts on professional social media websites such as LinkedIn can also be very effective. Be confident in reaching out to interesting people who are potentially key contacts. Start out by following them and reacting to their posts, posting your own blog or article on the same subject area and so, when you do finally reach out to them you are not quite so 'cold' but already part of their circle.

At the same time, you can, of course, read job adverts for information about the requirements of positions. This can be helpful to compare and check that your qualifications and experience match with what firms are looking for. Make sure to get job alerts from job sites. While we're on the subject: update your LinkedIn profile to reflect what you have to offer specifically, as recruiters (both in-house and external firms) are always on the lookout for suitable talent and all use LinkedIn. LinkedIn offers good tutorials on how to create an effective profile, and it is worth the time to do this properly.

There are so many opportunities now to make new contacts in addition to mining your previous ones, and people are usually very willing to share experiences and information; so start your focused networking now!

For your journal

1. Draw up a list or a brainstorming map of contacts as you work through your columns of opportunity table and match the places you want to find out more about with the people who can help you do this.
2. Create a spreadsheet with your contacts' details, the dates you contacted them, and the outcome.
3. Begin to reach out to the contacts you have identified as useful sources of information.
4. Update your LinkedIn profile with a catchy and attractive statement about yourself and what you have to offer.
5. Systematically follow key people on LinkedIn and begin to engage with them proactively.
6. Join social apps and forums to find new contacts in the areas you are interested in; be proactive and reach out to them.
7. Prepare and practise your 'pitch' to be able to tell people exactly what expertise you offer that puts you apart from everyone else, preferably in less than five words.

RETURNING TO WORK AFTER SOME TIME OUT

Fact – women are more likely to take time out from their career than men. They are most often the ones who give up their career or go part-time to bring up children or take on other caring responsibilities; and this is very often due to the still prevalent gender pay gap. There are couples where both parents take parental leave, but this is relatively rare in practice and companies still react with surprise when a future father requests paternity leave, even when it is contractually agreed. And staying away from work for the first months or year of a baby's life is only the beginning. You then need to find good, affordable childcare for the period that follows, which is not always easy. Again, it is more often the mother who puts off returning to her career.

Perhaps you are considering a return to the same work after a career break or you feel that you would now like something new and are toying with the idea of a career change. Whichever path you choose, this is an exciting place to be, full of opportunities ready to be grasped if you know how to navigate the process.

Let's take a look at two women who were at a career crossroads in their lives after having children and what road they chose. Lorna and Pamela took quite different lengths of time out of their career when they had children.

Case study

Lorna had a Master's degree in Environmental Science from a European university and an MBA from Harvard University. She worked for a management consulting company before and in the early part of her marriage but then gave up her job when she had two children. Lorna had devoted herself to her children and supporting her husband for six years, but once she had settled the children in day care and kindergarten, Lorna was ready to return to work.

Although she had been out of the workforce for six years, she wanted very much to return to work in her area of environmental protection and climate change and to pick up her career again at the level she left it. She also realised she wanted this to be the right career step and not a stop-gap. She was therefore prepared to wait and be discerning about which position she accepted and did her research very thoroughly, using her network astutely.

She was eventually offered the position of head of the newly founded corporate sustainability department of the holding company of a national transport company, an ideal match with her qualifications and her career aspirations.

Case study

Pamela had trained as a secondary school teacher, a job she loved, teaching English and history, but she only found a position at a school nearly 50 miles from where she lived. So, when her first child came along she gave up her job, hoping she would find a more convenient school closer to home when she returned from maternity leave. In fact, she then had two more children, each two years apart. She did some supply teaching while the children were small, but her youngest child had some learning difficulties and Pamela believed he needed more intensive care so she remained at home for a few more years. Her husband was more than happy for her to stay at home, and there was little discussion about the matter, which came about more by default than by active decision-making.

After 10 years, the idea of returning to a full-time teaching position seemed quite daunting, and Pamela felt she could not face a new curriculum and staffing regulations. She had also had a taste of schools from the perspective of a parent and had been less than happy with her experience.

Pamela was a devout Christian and had been involved with her local church on a voluntary basis for many years. When she started to reflect seriously about her professional future, acutely aware that the years were rushing by, she was pulled towards teaching mainly due to her past experience, but she knew she did not want to be part of the official education system.

Pamela relates easily to people, is a very good listener, and keenly sensitive to other people's needs. She has a caring personality with a strong sense of purpose and, although a mild-mannered person, is fierce about her convictions. She is also a good organiser.

A conversation with her parish priest led her to research potential opportunities to work within and for the church, and she discovered a range of opportunities, all of which would require re-training, but many of which had some connection with her previous work teaching young people. First, she committed herself to working on a regular basis in a volunteer capacity in the young people's counselling service, to get a feel for the role, and subsequently she trained as a lay-person church counsellor. For the last 16 years, she has worked in the counselling service and organised and ran retreats.

Pamela loves her work, which she finds fulfilling. She feels she could not have found a better way to use her many talents. She has never regretted not returning to teaching.

What do these two women have in common? Above all, resilience and a determination to be true to themselves in their search for the 'right' job in returning to their professional lives – as well as a flexibility and openness to new opportunities and settings for applying their skills. They were both fully aware that they needed to be proactive and keep an open mind to find a solution that would work for them and their families.

Preparing to put yourself forward

When it comes to actually applying for roles, there are practical steps you can take to prepare your CV and cover letter to ensure that you're always presenting your experience and qualities in the most effective way to be successful. In your toolkit, you'll find various activities that will help you to write the best possible CV, cover letter, and/or letter of interest.

A NOTE ON MANAGING EXPECTATIONS AND BEING KIND TO YOURSELF

Whichever transition path you're on, it's important you're able to manage your own expectations of the process and exercise some self-compassion along the way – not least if things don't unfold exactly as planned or on your preferred timeframe.

Keep hold of that positive growth mindset and a degree of flexibility to move and adapt to each challenge or opportunity as it arises. Often, it's the things you don't expect that can lead you to where you want to be!

Lorna and Pamela both faced challenges in the return to their careers as their expectations of the transition and those of their partners did not always match up. By being honest with yourself and open about what you want, you can try to manage both your own expectations and those of the people around you, especially your partners and families. Remember, it is not always a speedy process, as the rest of Lorna's story shows.

Case study

Lorna took nearly two years to complete her career transition. She first tried out a consultancy position in an international company, only to discover that she was not using her professional expertise in the way she had been led to expect she would. She found that she was acting more as the personal assistant to the department head and was given hardly any substantive work on sustainability issues.

When she left there to join the sustainability department of a national rail transport company, she was excited at the opportunity, but wary of whether this would turn out to be any different. Her main challenge turned out to be how to make the rest of the company accept that the Corporate Social Responsibility (CSR) department had value, as it was seen within the company as a nice-to-have decoration without much substance.

Lorna's transition back into professional work was thus something of a trial by fire, and she struggled to establish her role as head of CSR within the company – the setting up of the new department had been a political decision that was not welcomed by all. She put in long hours, which made her family life more difficult, as her husband also had an important position as the CFO of a global energy company.

Although he knew from the outset that Lorna wanted a professional life and a career for herself, somewhere deep down he had not quite believed that she would go through with this once they had children. A traditionalist at heart, he also had the backing of his parents, who lived in the same town and were opposed to Lorna working full time and leaving the children with carers.

Lorna thus had to face challenges on two fronts: at work and at home; but both Lorna and her husband had well-paying jobs, which meant they were able to pay for a lot of help, which made life easier. Over time, Lorna's husband saw how much her professional life meant to her and came round to not only accepting this but actively supporting her career ambitions.

Does anything in life ever unfold quite as perfectly and seamlessly as we'd like? Will there always be something – or someone – tugging at one's sleeve? Lorna's case study illustrates well the continuing plight of being a woman: that society has not yet created a totally level playing field and that we are often still torn between our separate identities. Yet, it is worth noting that, with a bit of patience and resilience, Lorna was still able to carefully navigate her way through these challenges to find fulfilment given the circumstances she faced.

Whatever the challenges you face as you make your own career transition, remember that you have the skills, abilities, and experience to carry you through – combined with a little determination, resilience, and a growth mindset you'll be well on your way to fulfilling your goals and ambitions.

For your journal

1. Reflect on how you will manage your expectations and those of the people closest to you.
2. How much do/did you feel fulfilled in your current or previous work? (Scale of 1–10)
3. How much would you like to stay in the same area of work? (Scale of 1–10)
4. How much would you like to try out something different? (Scale of 1–10)
5. Can you name the three things that are most important to you for your next career phase?
6. What would you like to spend your days doing, ideally?

With the answers in front of you, you will have a sense of where you want to go next and should feel strengthened to begin your research, explore options for your journey, and to set out on your chosen path. The only way is up!

LEARNING THE NEW

8

When you start a new job or a new role in the same company, you are excited, curious, and determined to make a successful transition. You are also probably slightly anxious, but mainly hopeful and optimistic. As an employee, you enter an unfamiliar place where you need to learn not only the ropes of the day-to-day business but also the subtext of the organisational culture. You must learn to understand and work with the sometimes seemingly conflicting demands of colleagues, peers, and managers, some of whom may have hidden agendas. You have become a player in a complex system over which you have no control.

As a new employee, you have been hired because you show potential, but you still have to prove your worth and you must perform to the best of your ability as your performance will be evaluated (all companies do some kind of evaluation).

Good performance, however, is not necessarily enough to move you forward in your career and to think this is true is a big mistake. Now is the time to become aware of all the factors in addition to your performance that affect your career path: understanding the organisational culture and how you fit in, recognising how talent management is handled including what support you will get, understanding how to gain the right kind of experience that will position you for your next career step, and working out who will be the best contacts to build a relationship with.

If you have chosen to be self-employed, you are faced with a new environment where being out on your own is invigorating and empowering while at the same time being presented with a

DOI: 10.4324/9781003353720-12

new set of challenges. To establish yourself in the own-business scenario, it is not enough to be an expert in your area; you need to work on developing your business development skills, thinking strategically (thinking ahead and around corners, foreseeing potential obstacles and ways to overcome them), and financial planning. If and when you grow you may also want to think about setting up a team of associates to outsource tasks and for support when needed, and of course, there's the minor business of creating and growing a client base and forging and maintaining good relationships with sponsors and potential customers.

First, what do you need to do to understand your new environment? In many ways it's quite similar to those considerations discussed above for employees, only now you have to make these things happen for yourself. You need to understand and find the contacts you think will help you develop your business, you need to understand the culture and requirements of clients you want to work with, and you need to understand the overall landscape for freelancers or small businesses operating in your space. Basically, you need to gather the information easily, get involved with any groups and networking events, and start making things happen. As your own boss, your mindset *has* to be different. You're not tied to any rules as such, but you need to understand the space you need to navigate to move forward, and you need to be intentional and proactive at all times.

In addition to the practical elements of being the boss (registering and setting yourself up, business development, invoicing, tax returns, etc.), think especially about your attitude and approach. Are you confident that you can send the right message to clients? Take a look at Part 4 on Believing in Yourself.

LEARNING ABOUT YOUR ENVIRONMENT – GETTING THE FULL PICTURE

You've arrived and you know what you need to find out, but how do you go about actually making this happen? This is not as obvious as it sounds. Many people who move into a new company do not spend enough time finding out about how it works as a whole but concentrate only on the tasks they are assigned – which is fine but ideally you need to do both. You need to think macro (the bigger picture of the organisation as a whole) and micro (your individual role and its related tasks).

Indeed, while at first, it might seem less important than the day-to-day tasks required of your role, insight into the company's business will allow you to begin to understand how the company is structured, what the business interests and areas are, and how you might better contribute in your role. It's also a good idea to do some research in your private time on other companies in the industry. What are the similarities; what are the differences? Developing a firm understanding of where your company sits in the competitor landscape is a great way of understanding what its strategic priorities might be.

It is also important to spend some time considering the organisational culture of the company: is it hierarchical or flat, formal or informal? How approachable are managers and senior leaders? Is your manager interested in their team members as people? Is your manager interested in your career development? If the company is going through change, how is this change communicated by senior management? How diverse is the workforce? Is there a positive attitude towards cultural diversity? How important is this to you?

Your awareness of the kind of company you are in will help you make an informed decision about where the opportunities lie and how long to stay there, as well as how compatible your career choice to date is with your values and career aspirations. This will all help you to make valid comparisons with other companies when you start to look around.

Now you know... is it still the right fit for you?

As you learn more about your new company, you are also learning how you fit within it and whether the role you have is a good match for your career aspirations. One coachee of mine made a very deliberate move from the public to the private sector because she wanted to find out whether in her area, corporate learning, there were new things that the private sector was doing and whether the working environment would be a good match for her. After less than a year, she knew not only that the private sector had no new tricks but that her home was in the international public sector. It was a rich learning experience.

Rosemary, in my next case study, realised during her training period with a company that the role she was being prepared for was actually not the best fit for her and was able, through careful negotiations and support from her manager, to change direction.

Case study

Rosemary had entered the graduate management scheme of a national retailer with many branches. In addition to her management training, she moved from one department to another, spending time in the retail outlets and back of store and also at headquarters. She got to know all the departments and many specific jobs – invaluable experience for a future manager. But Rosemary learned something about herself as well; she realised she did not want to stay on the store manager career track but was more interested in working at headquarters and specifically moving into marketing/branding. After her store management training, with support from her manager, she transferred to headquarters and began work in the marketing department for which she was given training both on the job and in marketing courses.

If you are not given the opportunity to experience areas in the company other than your own, try to meet people from other departments and find out what they do. In this way, you can gain an overview of the many parts of a company and how they fit together.

LEARNING THE NEW SELF-EMPLOYED ENVIRONMENT

Transitioning into the own-business scenario also requires a level of learning about your environment; only for the new business owner or freelancer, the focus will be on how your industry works in a freelance/consultancy setting and how to go about building a client base and creating a business relationship with each new client. Both are key to a successful transition.

Try to find and reach out to people in a similar situation; they may be your competitors, but you will find that most people are willing to share their knowledge about the ropes of their industry. Visit industry forums and events, chats, social media buzzes, and LinkedIn feeds, which are all valuable sources of information. Join a support association – look for ones aimed at the self-employed and entrepreneurs in particular – where you can meet with those facing the same obstacles and challenges and who may well already have some of the answers you're looking for.

Probably the biggest mistake you can make when setting up on your own is to think you can do it all alone – while you can certainly try, you are better to identify where your strengths are and focus on that work and bring in support for other time-consuming areas that an expert could handle much more quickly and easily (such as accounting).

When it comes to the matter of finding your first clients, if you're not already clear on exactly who you want to target then using your new network and talking to people in a similar situation can help you to find out what kind of potential clients hire people with your skills. Then, you can do your own market research to learn what these potential clients are looking for before making your initial approach.

Before you do this, make sure you learn everything you can about them. Read the information they put out about themselves on their website, etc.; see what you can find in the media and on social media about them. You need to understand *exactly* what they are trying to achieve so that you can then understand *exactly* what they need in the form of extra help to achieve this, and then pitch yourself in a way as to show that you are *the* person to do this for them.

When you get that initial meeting, do not be afraid to ask your potential client questions directly. This shows initiative and business acumen and proves you are really interested in providing the best possible customer service to them.

For your journal

1. Make a list of the information you need and where you hope to find it:

    a. organisational/industry literature and publications
    b. intranet and internet
    c. people who can give you the information you need.

2. Join an industry forum or support association.
3. Draw up a template questionnaire to find out about business partners and clients.
4. Make a list of potential clients (i.e. client groups and then individual clients) and categorise them according to business areas, their interests and how you can best provide what they need.

MAKING FRIENDS WITH THE LEGACY OF YOUR PREDECESSOR

Transitioning into a new role in an organisation often means that you are taking the place of someone who has left. You may be fortunate enough to have a clear and orderly handover and receive induction by your predecessor. All too often though, this is not the case and what you learn about your predecessor are snippets, asides, brief comparisons, or silence. If you can break through this silence and glean some concrete information about the person who used to do your job, this can be very helpful, because one of the most overlooked challenges in a transition phase is confronting the legacy of the person who sat in your chair before you. In one scenario, this was a much-loved colleague, a super team player, and a first-rate, creative worker who always delivered on time. You might feel that you can only pale in comparison. Even if this is a picture seen through rose-tinted spectacles, this is the picture you have to contend with as everyone is sad at losing their former colleague and may even resent that they now have to cope with someone new. They may doubt your ability to fill their former colleague's shoes. You can counter such suspicion by making your admiration known: express how pleased you are to be able to build on your predecessor's achievements.

In the opposite scenario, everyone is glad to have seen the back of the person in question. Does this mean they have high hopes for you and welcome you with open arms? Not necessarily. They may have become resigned to the situation and still be very cautious in their attitude.

The third scenario lies somewhere in the middle. Ambivalent or neutral feelings towards the former colleague will result in a waiting attitude towards you.

It is important as the newcomer to take the time to learn about the people as well as the way things are done. If you have a managerial role, your team needs to feel that you are willing to learn the ropes and respect the set rules because that shows respect for them and the previous leader. The following example of Catherine, who ignored the good work that her predecessor had accomplished with the team and saw only the things that needed changing, shows how damaging misjudging a situation can be.

Case study

Catherine was hired to a coordinator position in an academy when the former incumbent retired. He had been in that position for many years and was universally liked by both teaching and administrative staff, and by the students too. He had a reputation for always finding a compromise solution, which was in the best interests of the protagonists, even if he sometimes had to re-interpret the rules. His door was always open. He was also disorganised, constantly overworked, and behind on many administrative deadlines, which sometimes threatened to have alarming consequences for the institution. Catherine was determined to sweep clean: she tightened up administrative procedures and deadlines; she set office hours and adhered to them; she introduced new policies and was strict and inflexible in applying the rules and regulations; her door was always closed. The new regime arrived with a vengeance and the result was resistance from nearly all sides. It took Catherine nearly a year of coaching to accept and undo her mistakes and put the department back on track.

Catherine didn't understand that her team needed to go through their own period of transition to enable them to accept her and her new ideas. She didn't take the time to learn how to communicate with them, to listen to their stories of their achievements with the previous boss, and to create a relationship with them. This would have been the best approach to gradually get the team on board with her ideas. When anyone leaves a position they have held for a long period of time, the new incumbent must acknowledge the feelings of those left and show respect for the predecessor by allowing colleagues time and space for what is in effect a period of mourning. In this case, they had lost not only a colleague but also a friend. Had Catherine realised the importance of this transition phase, she would have trodden softly and had a far greater chance of success earlier on.

A better approach was taken by Sirin.

Case study

Sirin faced a difficult situation when she started her first job as a junior manager leading a well-established team whose manager had left for a job at a competitor organisation. She told the team that she wanted to get to know them and hoped to get on well with them all. She went out of her way to create opportunities where this would be possible in a slightly informal manner, organising, for example, Friday coffee breaks for which she brought in fresh fruit and muffins at her own expense. Although the team seemed to appreciate Sirin's approach, at least on the surface, after a couple of months, she realised that all was not well and that two factions had formed. One group was subverting the work of the other and petty conflicts broke out, information was not shared, documents were filed where they could only be found after a long search, time was wasted, and tempers flared. Sirin realised that this could not go on and she reserved a Friday afternoon to have a team meeting to sort out the problem.

At this meeting, it became clear that the one group had not got over the loss of their previous manager and felt that Sirin had introduced too many changes too fast. Sirin knew that, objectively, this was not true, but she had to work with the fact that this was how some of her team perceived it. First, she took pains to acknowledge the contribution that the previous manager had made, which released the tension at the meeting, and the whole team then set to work to resolve the complaints. Sirin made it clear that there were certain innovations that the company required, but then showed flexibility in how these would be introduced. The result was a real coming together of the team, which laid the groundwork for productive work in the future.

Sirin resolved the issue of team morale, which was really due to the fact that some members of her team were struggling with the leadership transition. She spent time solving the problem with sensitivity, giving her team the chance to grieve openly about the loss of their former boss, enabling them to move on and begin to accept her.

For your journal

1. Reflect on past situations when you have been the new person in a new group; how did you gain their trust and create relationships?
2. Make a list of all the good things you notice in your first ten days about your new colleagues, their way of working, and what they achieved in the past. Make a point of mentioning some of the things to them.
3. Reflect on your communication skills: practise listening and prepare good questions to find out what people think.

ESTABLISHING CREDIBILITY

When you start in a new position, it is crucial to immediately begin to establish your credibility in order to be accepted into the team. If you are credible, people will begin to trust you, and trust is the foundation for all good working relationships and a productive and creative working environment. To establish credibility effectively, you need to focus on three main points.

1. Demonstrate your competence. Always be as well prepared as possible and deliver the highest standard of work you can on time.
2. Be honest. Sometimes you won't know the answer and you need to realise that that's okay. A coachee of mine, a really bright, hard-working, and competent young woman, was paralysed when starting a new job at the thought of being asked by her manager or at a meeting about something she didn't know the answer to. You can pre-empt that situation to some

extent by being well prepared for meetings but also accept that as the newbie you won't always have the answer – but that you can be willing to go find it out.

3. Be willing to learn. Show interest. Asking questions actually helps your credibility if they are intelligent and thought-provoking. Similarly, being willing to take on a new task that may be a little challenging proves that you want to establish yourself as a full member of the team.

As a new freelancer or business owner, you are constantly answering the question 'Why me?' Why should a prospective client or customer choose you over another supplier? The answer is only partially the quality or the innovative nature of the product or service you offer; you also have to establish your credibility and trustworthiness to your clients, associates, supporters, donors, regulators, and suppliers. So, in addition to the top three ways of establishing credibility generally, you should pay attention to three more things.

1. Demonstrate your credibility by leveraging past sources of legitimacy, i.e. your references and testimonials. Of course, this is easier if you have become a consultant for an organisation with whom you worked previously in-house; so, it is all the more important if that is not the case for you to nevertheless demonstrate positive feedback for your product/service and yourself.

2. Show that you're trustworthy and reliable; always return calls and emails; be proactive with information and ideas; deliver on time; follow up immediately on queries or requests for changes.

3. Recognise your audience's expectations; repeat them back to demonstrate that you have heard what they expect of you and state how you will fulfil those expectations. In essence, meet them where they are and show you understand them and that you can give them exactly what they need (note that they may not yet know what they need, it's your job to identify this and explain it to them).

DEVELOPING AN APPROPRIATE WORK STYLE

Work processes and office culture vary from workplace to workplace and from team to team (depending on the manager), and you may need to adapt your own work style to your new working environment in order to fit in. Sometimes this can be something as basic as providing more frequent progress reports or being flexible in responding to requests from different time zones if your new company works globally. But you may need to adapt more fundamentally; for example, you may need to learn to be adaptable if your new team has a more open and flexible approach to the working day and you are accustomed to structuring your day quite strictly (or vice versa!). This can be quite a shift in work style to accommodate interruptions and requests for ad hoc meetings.

Teleworking is here to stay in some form or another, so a culture of virtual meetings is one to watch out for in your new workplace. As organisations are working out how they want their employees to work in offices in a post-pandemic world, you may need to adapt again to new requirements.

When you transition from being an employee or staff member to working independently, your horizon widens dramatically; the single focus becomes a wide-angled perspective, and this will likely have consequences for your work style. As an independent worker, you are the one who designs, plans, and implements, and, if you have associates or staff, you must also delegate, motivate, and monitor. This kind of responsibility requires a rigorous attitude to one's own commitments and a skilful use of one's own resources. Time management and prioritisation are prime skills and a tendency to procrastinate will not be helpful. You need to be able to function under pressure sometimes and then be able to switch off to recuperate. You must see the bigger picture and also have a close eye to detail.

It is helpful to be flexible and willing to adapt when necessary. You need to have your vision of your business always in your mind's eye and yet be able to target individual goals and be detail-oriented, to be thorough but also take decisions swiftly. One of my clients had a wonderful mentor from whom she learned that being the boss also means accepting that some things can't be pushed through. You will give it your all, but you also have to recognise when you can't go any further and have to walk away.

The freelancer or business owner must be prepared to confront problems and not be afraid of them – problems will always exist and when working independently, there is no escalation point to pass the issue on to. All this doesn't mean you should not listen to others' opinions; on the contrary, it is important to keep your mind open to ways of doing things that may be new or different, as no one operates well in an echo chamber. If your default work style is independent hard work and you are more comfortable doing things alone and being self-reliant, when you become the boss, it is important to balance that with an objective perspective to test your ideas. Sometimes a business partner or associate can provide exactly that balance.

For your journal

1. Reflect on your work style and consider what and how you need to adapt
2. Schedule time for time management and strategic planning in your diary

9

THE PEOPLE FACTOR

UNDERSTANDING OTHER PEOPLE'S BEHAVIOUR WITH EMOTIONAL INTELLIGENCE

A career transition of any kind means getting to know and work with new people: colleagues, managers, and clients. We are sometimes surprised at the way people behave because we tend to be stuck in our own way of thinking how things 'should' be done and struggle to put ourselves in the shoes of others.

When we move into a new work environment, we must be prepared for others to act and react in ways that are different from our own and from how people behaved in our previous workplace. Being aware of ourselves helps us to understand others. Psychometric tests can help you get to know your personality and default behaviour preferences better, but you don't even really need them if you just watch yourself and others in the workplace and try to understand what drives your feelings, choices, and approaches to certain tasks.

How do you react, for example, to a request to research a subject by a deadline? Do you begin methodically with a list of possible information sources and another list of sub-topics? Do you proceed to look up the sources one-by-one, ticking off each when you have retrieved the information? Or do you start by brainstorming everything you can think of about the subject, allowing your mind to wander freely, thinking outside the box, and being as inventive as you can?

Both approaches are valid, but they are just different. If your default position is the former, you might dismiss the colleague

DOI: 10.4324/9781003353720-13

who works to the latter as wasting time, but in fact, they might come up with some fresh ideas which make the subject richer. This is why teams with a diverse mix of skills, work styles, and personalities are more effective than uniform teams. Each team member contributes something different to a project or problem and together they are more creative. Simply by reaching out to a colleague to show you appreciate their way of doing something can make a connection.

You can improve your interactions with all the people you come into contact with by taking their feelings into account and using your emotional intelligence. In essence, in order to relate well to other people, you first need to recognise and understand your own emotions and then learn to manage these. Once you have reached that level of emotional intelligence, you can become aware of other people's emotions and come to manage your relationships better. It is not easy to think or talk about emotions in a professional context, but we are all human beings and not robots, we do not leave our feelings at the entrance to the office building (or the virtual office) and pick them up on our way home. It is therefore worthwhile taking your co-workers' feelings and perspectives into consideration in the hope of improving your workplace relations. A really helpful approach is to 'put yourself in a colleague's shoes' before you make a judgement or assume something about them or their motives.

For your journal

1. Have you ever had a misunderstanding with a colleague, perhaps because you misread how they were feeling?
2. Have you ever felt misunderstood by a colleague and, if so, what could you have done to improve the situation?
3. Reflect on an incident at work from a different perspective to fully understand how one project/event/conversation could be interpreted very differently by someone else. Put yourself 'in the other person's shoes' and see how it feels to be them. Activities to support this can be found in your toolkit.

TEAMWORK – BUILDING TRUST

Think of any sports team: a racing sailboat team, a climbing team, a relay team. Every team is based on mutual trust. We all know how hard it is to trust someone you don't know, and yet that is exactly what we are asked to do when we join a new team and, to be honest, this can't happen overnight. You need to build trust gradually to be accepted in the team and for your colleagues to feel they can rely on you – and vice versa! So, how can you build relationships which will allow your colleagues to trust you and you to trust them?

The first thing to do is to show interest in your colleagues and demonstrate respect for their knowledge and expertise, and also show you are willing to learn from them. Use every opportunity to demonstrate that they can rely on you by delivering work on time and supporting someone if they ask.

When I work with teams in team-building workshops to improve their team cohesion and performance, the top concern is always how to improve communication within the team and between the team leader and the team. Teams suffer greatly from people who keep information to themselves or only partly share information; so, as the newest team member, make sure to keep your colleagues informed about your progress on tasks and projects in which they are involved. This also means being honest when you need help or don't manage to complete something on time.

When you work closely with someone else, always include and mention their contribution when you talk about the project to others and give your colleagues credit for the work they have done. This, too, builds trust between you, whereas not doing so damages their trust in you. As a new team member, you may be tempted to try to get yourself noticed by your team leader, but never undermine a colleague's contribution by emphasising only your own.

It is also a good idea to participate in social activities where possible because you are demonstrating that you want to bond with your colleagues. Try to fit in with team rituals. If everyone goes for a drink on Friday at 5 pm, then try to go too, at least sometimes. Of course, this may not always work for you; perhaps your personal life doesn't facilitate much socialising, or you don't feel comfortable in social situations. Nevertheless, try to show up occasionally. Out-of-office conversations can be useful, in addition to showing solidarity. There are activities to support you in building trust in your toolkit.

For your journal

1. Reflect on how you learned to trust someone at work. What did they do to gain your trust?
2. Make a list of the ways in which you helped or supported a colleague in the past.
3. Reflect on how you would build a new team's trust in you.

BUILDING A RELATIONSHIP WITH YOUR NEW MANAGER

Learning to handle the relationship with your new manager is one of the most useful strategic professional skills you can learn for every career transition you will make. Not only is the one-to-one relationship at stake but your manager can also be instrumental in consolidating your position in the company and in supporting you to prepare for your next career step.

Some managers are easy-going, team-oriented, and generally keen to make life for their staff as pleasant as possible. Others may be distant or demanding. Rarely, fortunately, will you find 'horrible bosses' who allow themselves tantrums, rudeness, or abusive behaviour. If the company permits such a manager, it will be best to leave as soon as possible for your own safety. You will gain nothing from that situation, and, sadly, it is often daunting to lodge a complaint and follow through, although most organisations encourage a 'speak-up' culture. If you do not feel able to complain and follow through, the best course of action is to leave and make your reasons clear to the HR director upon departure.

Your manager's goal is to ensure that the work is done to a satisfactory standard. In order to achieve this goal, a manager will in principle be keen to motivate their team to perform to the best of their ability. But sometimes managers are overworked and stressed and overlook the importance of on-boarding a new employee to make them feel part of the team.

Case study

When Hallie joined the five-person compliance team of a global mining corporation, she was determined to shine in her new job and made every effort to show her manager, Luiz, how competent she was. However, she frequently found it difficult to catch up with him, as he was often absent attending meetings, and even when he was in the office, he had little time for her. Hallie tried sending him emails to get his feedback on her progress but seldom received a reply. She became increasingly despondent, because she had hoped for a supportive manager who made time for her, and who would act as a mentor, whereas Luiz restricted his interactions with her to a minimum, only sending her emails about tasks and often ignoring her in the irregularly held team meetings.

Take a moment to consider your manager's challenges: targets to meet, deadlines to adhere to, budgets to monitor, and regulations to comply with. In addition, a manager has to 'manage' a number of people, each with their own cultural background, talents, character traits, skills and shortcomings, personal problems, and career aspirations: in a word, emotional and psychological baggage. This is a tricky juggling act.

Every member of staff would like their manager's attention. As the newest team member, Hallie's main objective should be to fit in, not stand out. She needed to figure out how best to support Luiz and the rest of the team. Hallie made the forgivable mistake of thinking about herself first, where it would have been more helpful to consider what Luiz needed. He was overworked, running an important section with a relatively small team, and it was not his style or custom to devote a lot of time to new recruits. This is sometimes the case, however regrettable.

Case study

Hallie's task was to find a way of working with him which would first fulfil his needs without ignoring her own. In our coaching sessions, Hallie decided to request a meeting with Luiz dedicated to their way of working together. She identified what she felt she needed from Luiz and how to present this to him in the meeting, but she planned to ask him first how he wanted to work with her and how she could best support him, what communication methods he would like her to use and how often he wanted her to check in about her progress. At the meeting, Hallie and Luiz came to an understanding about working together which included a weekly progress report email from Hallie that Luiz would respond to.

Hallie felt better after the meeting, although in fact, Luiz did not always respond to her weekly reports as fully as she would have liked. Hallie learned an important lesson: she was the one who needed to adapt to her manager's work style, not the other way round. Hallie came to accept that Luiz was not the manager to mentor her in the way that she would have liked and so she found a mentor in another part of the organisation who helped her settle in and supported her through her transition into the company. (More about mentors later.)

Your manager has their own culture of communication which you should try to comply with. Is there an open-door policy? Can you use a weekly team meeting to ask questions and raise issues? Is email the right way to communicate with your manager or can you phone or send a text message? Is it okay to stop them in the corridor? Are you expected to provide progress reports? In writing or in person? How long? How often?

It is your responsibility to keep your manager informed about your progress on tasks – again, with awareness of the level of information required. In this way, you are making their job easier.

For your journal

Plan your initial meeting with your new manager meticulously. You need to find out how they work and how they want you to work with them.

1. Summarise for yourself what you already know.
2. Prepare a list of questions.

   a. What are your work priorities?
   b. How often does the manager want an update on your progress, any substantive changes, unexpected developments and results, etc.?
   c. How would your manager like you to communicate with them (email, WhatsApp, face-to-face, etc.)?
   d. Who in the team should you work most closely with; is there a 'work buddy' system, if not could you nevertheless have one colleague to whom you could turn for support?
   e. How often do team meetings take place and how are they conducted?
   f. How can you best support your manager/the team?
   g. What is most important for you to learn/develop first?

3. Request a meeting after a couple of months to discuss your progress and career development options. At that meeting, you can identify a special assignment to develop a skill.

BUILDING A RELATIONSHIP WITH YOUR TEAM AS THE NEW MANAGER OR BOSS

When you become a manager, your goal is to build a constructive and positive relationship with each member of your team and, again, you can only do this by building up mutual trust.

Begin by enlisting their support. The best way to do this is to ask questions: about themselves, their work, and how they feel the team is doing. Although this may seem obvious, it is not always practised; some new managers come in with, as they think, all the answers. Christine Lagarde once gave an interview in which she said that when she became the head of the IMF, she did not know a great deal about the job, but that she was very good at asking questions.

Talk to each member of your team individually and also with the team as a whole so that you can begin to get to know each of them on a one-to-one basis and also to understand their dynamic as a group. Be transparent about what you are doing when you ask each one to come to your office for a short talk about their work. Before the meetings, find out as much as you can about each team member from past evaluations, work submitted, results, etc. Have a basic plan for the meeting, and ask the following types of questions:

1. What does your work plan look like at the moment?
2. Are there any areas of work/tasks/type of assignments which you particularly enjoy doing?
3. How do you see the team working together?
4. Do you have any difficulties you would like to share with me?
5. Do you have any ideas on improving our work?
6. Is there anything else you would like me to know?

Say that you hope you will work well together and that the staff member should come to you with any concerns and also with any good ideas.

The first team meetings set the tone for all future ones, so encourage people to talk openly, ask questions, and say what is on their mind. The sign of a good team meeting is when the team members talk more than you do!

You will probably get only part of the picture in the beginning. Do not expect people to be completely open with you from the word go. It will take time for your team to learn to trust you, but you can begin to build up that trust by sharing all relevant information with them and being transparent about what is happening in the organisation. However, openness and a willingness to share (especially with a manager) are culturally determined and subject to individual preferences. Whereas some cultures encourage openness and honesty, others believe strongly in privacy and reserve, and part of your challenge as a manager will be to find out the truth below the layers of politeness and acquiescence with which you are met.

One of the greatest skills as a manager is to be able to build trust with and in your team and all the people you interact with including, of course, your customers or clients. Trust is closely linked with the concept of psychological safety at work, which means that everyone feels safe enough to speak up, share concerns, or make a mistake without fear of negative repercussions.

This applies equally to the self-employed scenario: you will have people with whom you collaborate and those to whom you delegate or outsource tasks and you have to create a sense in all these people that they can trust you – and that you trust them! They must be certain that they can rely on you and that you will fulfil what you undertake to do and that you are really all pulling together as one team. The bonds between you as the boss and your associates are in theory not as strong as those in an employer–employee setting and so must be nurtured and strengthened over time.

One way in which to build trust and team loyalty is to encourage 'black box' thinking, which means openly talking about what happened when a mistake was made and how to ensure it won't happen again. As the manager or the boss, it is up to you to create a non-judgemental atmosphere so that your team feel it is safe to admit mistakes and raise concerns if they notice something is not right. In this way, you can work at avoiding problems.

For your journal

1. Initial meetings with your team members are an important opportunity to make a first impression and to begin to pick up information about the individuals and about the team as a whole, so set up individual meetings as well as team meetings to begin to get to know each of them on a one-to-one basis. A successful meeting is one where your team member talks more than you do!

2. Before the individual meetings, find out as much as you can about each team member from past evaluations, work submitted, results, etc.

3. Schedule the meeting either face-to-face or virtually with enough time for the conversation; be present and engaged (turn off email and phone alerts).

4. Have a basic plan for the meeting and ask the following kind of questions:

   a. What does your work plan look like now?
   b. Are there any areas of work/tasks/type of assignments which you particularly enjoy doing?
   c. What areas would you like to do more of?
   d. How do you see the team working together?
   e. Do you have any difficulties you would like to share with me?
   f. Do you have any ideas on improving our work?
   g. Is there anything else you would like me to know?
   h. Say that you hope you will work well together and that they can always come to you with any concerns and with any good ideas.

In the toolkit, you will find an additional exercise "Mapping My New Team".

10

COMMUNICATION SKILLS – COMMUNICATING FOR PURPOSE

COMMUNICATING EFFECTIVELY

When you make a career move, consider the communication culture of your new context and whether you need to adapt the way you communicate in your new position. This is all the more important if you have moved to a managerial role or have become your own boss: you are the communications chief and spokesperson. What you say and how you say it will be noticed. Right from the moment you start in your new role, you need to send the right message about yourself. Traditionally, a difference has been made between two distinct types of communication culture. The directive, transactional type lays emphasis on clear and direct guidelines or orders and is a 'telling' culture, whereas the relational type relies more on emotional intelligence and is a 'coaching' culture in which feedback in both directions is welcome. But your communication is most effective when you combine the two types to create a culture that makes all interactions run more smoothly and results in a good working atmosphere. The best teams regard communication as an open market where comments, input, suggestions, feedback, and ideas are always welcome and a 'speak-up' culture is encouraged, and the opinions of others are respected.

If you communicate well in your new role, you can position yourself as someone with a future; your good work gets you noticed, of course, but so does how you relate to and communicate with all the different people with whom you interact. Good

DOI: 10.4324/9781003353720-14

communication is good self-advertisement, so here are a few ways to improve your communication skills.

When we talk, we believe we are communicating, but our communication is not always effective. In the gap between what we say and what the listener understands, many things can interfere with our message being received in the way that we intended. Our listener's attention may be elsewhere; they may have assumed something which prevents them from following our train of thought; they may have made assumptions about us, which makes it difficult for them to listen to what we are saying, or they may have a very different view of the situation or see it through a different prism (cultural differences often lead to misunderstandings).

Consider how your listeners are feeling. What state of mind are they in? Are they tired, or stressed, or rushed? Is this a good moment to say what you want to say? How much attention can they pay to your message? Is the message itself difficult? If so, how will they want it to be delivered? In addition, consider their standpoint and reflect in advance what you could do to ensure you address their concerns and possible objections. Take a moment to consider the best channel for your message – email, telephone, in person? Many people feel overwhelmed by a number of on-screen meetings, so a simple phone call could be a refreshing change. What is the culture for communication in the company you have moved to? Many a new recruit has drawn unfavourable attention by not conforming to email etiquette. It may be that your company favours short and snappy emails for internal communications, but be aware that this may not be true for communications with clients and external counterparts. And most importantly, however you are feeling that day do not let your negative emotions show to anyone else.

The golden rule of putting yourself in your listener's shoes applies equally to meetings and presentations. What do they want and need to hear? How can you best grab and hold their attention? Be concise and to the point. Leave time for questions. Learn to think on your feet.

Communication is only partly about the message itself. It is also about the way that message is packaged: your tone of voice, the words and metaphors you use, and your body language. Particularly in a multi-cultural environment, we should watch our choice of words: slang phrases may be incomprehensible to someone with a different native language. Different cultural backgrounds can often be a barrier to good communication – here I mean not only national or ethnical backgrounds but also different work backgrounds and perspectives. For example, IT experts talk a language among themselves that they may need to adjust when explaining something to the rest of their organisation. Try to use the language others use when speaking to them, which will help them feel you understand them.

Women sometimes unconsciously try to soften their remarks by prefacing them with a qualifying phrase such as, 'Would you be so kind as to…', 'You know more about it than I do, but have you thought of…', 'This may not be the right moment, but…', 'I just wanted to suggest…'. All these may be perceived as uncertainty instead of politeness. Try always to give your opinion in a direct and focused way. Plan what you want to say, organise your thoughts and your words, and keep to the point. Listen to yourself and reflect later on how you communicated – be your own best critic and learn for the future.

Similarly, beware of apologising. Although it is, of course, right to apologise when you have made a mistake or hurt someone's feelings, avoid starting your sentences with phrases such as 'I'm sorry, but…', 'I'm afraid…', 'I hate to say it, but…', 'Forgive me, but…', 'I hope you don't mind my asking…'. It is better to just ask your question or make your statement. Often our speech patterns have been trained from an early age, and if you are in the habit of apologising you may be confusing a desire to be polite or empathetic with a need to apologise.

Practise ways of communicating which strengthen your position and the message you are sending; for example, do not allow someone to interrupt you when you are speaking. You can either raise your voice very slightly or pause for quiet and calmly say something like 'If I may just finish what I was saying' or 'I will just finish my thought'.

On the other hand, a communication strength is taking the time for a few remarks to set a comfortable tone for a discussion and make people feel at ease, something that became especially noticeable in online meetings during the Covid-19 pandemic.

People – and women especially – have described how they have suffered from the relentless on-screen, subject-focused meetings and have missed the 'in-between' conversations that take place in a real as opposed to a virtual conversation. Online meetings will continue to play a big role in working life, so we must learn how to handle them well, both technologically and emotionally. If the way you communicate establishes your competence and expertise, showing a human side, too, will make you a more congenial colleague, boss, and negotiating partner, and your colleagues and customers will appreciate your contributions all the more.

Communication checklist

1. Plan your communication. What do you want to get out of the conversation? What should be different at the end?
2. What do you think the other person wants to get out of the conversation? How interested are they in having the conversation? How will you make them interested? What's in it for them?
3. Plan the right time, place, and mode for the conversation.
4. Consider the other person's background, their culture, professional situation, and also their personal context.
5. Pick the person up from where they are standing; bring them closer to you and do not expect them to take the first step. Explain what's in it for them.
6. Practise really listening; then play back what you think you have heard.
7. Listen between 'the lines'.
8. Consider what language the other person speaks: English (native or not)..., IT..., business...., scientific..., marketing...., etc.
9. Use the other person's language as far as possible to help them feel you understand them better.
10. Have a (mental) checklist of the points you want to get across and how you want the conversation to go (talking points).
11. Stay focused on the topic of the conversation without digressing.
12. Check that the other person has understood you by asking them to paraphrase or summarise what they heard you say.
13. Also check back that you have understood your partner.
14. At the end of the conversation, summarise what you have agreed (action points).

For your journal

1. Use the communication skills checklist.
2. Reflect on your way of communicating and whether you have 'female' speech patterns.
3. Analyse what you said during a conversation or a meeting scenario as an exercise.
4. Try out different ways of communicating (phone call, email, online meeting, in-person conversation) and reflect on how each serves a purpose.
5. Plan an important conversation in advance, putting yourself mentally in your discussion partner's shoes.

RECEIVING FEEDBACK

It is quite difficult to be objective about our own performance or behaviour, but to transition successfully into a new role, we have to know how we are doing. Getting constructive feedback can be really helpful for your career development. Many organisations arrange for 360-degree feedback assessments for their employees as part of the performance evaluation process or talent development programme, and if your company does so, then this is a great opportunity to learn how others see you.

Case study

I coached Manuela after a 360-degree assessment in which she had received feedback from her manager, her four direct reports, four peers in the same department, and three other colleagues. She had started her job just a year previously, so this was the first formal evaluation after her career transition. In the self-assessment, Manuela had rated herself very highly in all the eight areas and her supervisor, too, had given her excellent ratings. But Manuela was surprised at the ratings she received from her peers and other colleagues who all rated her quite a bit lower than she had rated herself in communicating and delegating. There were several comments about her lack of clarity in giving directions and being impatient with results. Although Manuela believed she had been efficient in collaborating with other departments, she accepted that she had to improve the way she did so.

When someone gives us positive feedback, we feel wonderful – and we all need it, because we thrive upon recognition and rewards. It is a different story when someone criticises something that we did. This may be because we realise we didn't do a good job, or it may be how the feedback was given, the choice of words, or the tone of voice, or because others heard the comment. We feel awful.

It is worth taking a closer look at that feeling. What happens between the criticism being expressed and you feeling terrible? The criticism triggered something in you which led to a feeling of embarrassment, shame, or anger. Why? Why do we allow something that someone says to affect us in such a way? Perhaps you know you didn't come up to standard, so you are angry at yourself for not having done better. Perhaps you feel the criticism is not valid and are angry at the person delivering it, who is probably your boss, but possibly a colleague or a client.

It helps to try to see the criticism as constructive feedback about our action or behaviour and not about us as a person. Ideally, this is also the way that constructive feedback is best delivered, directed at the method or the outcome of what we did that was not up to standard or not appropriate. But even if this is not how the feedback was given, when we receive it we can try not to take it personally. In future, we must change the way we do this task, and, hopefully, the feedback also contained some guidance on how.

It is not easy, but we can learn to accept constructive feedback that helps us improve and grow at any time in our career.

For your journal

1. Ask for feedback about the way you handled a situation and analyse that feedback objectively.
2. When you receive feedback, reflect on how it made you feel and what you can learn from it.
3. Go back over similar situations and reflect on what you could have done differently; then be on the lookout for situations in which to put your insights into practice.

DEALING WITH UNACCEPTABLE BEHAVIOUR

The #MeToo movement finally brought out into the open behaviour which can unfortunately no longer be regarded as isolated, and which occurs in all types of industries and professions and in all sizes of organisations. Unfortunately, new recruits are more likely to be targets of harassment as the perpetrators abuse the fact that the new employee feels insecure in the organisation, doesn't know the ropes, and has no one to turn to.

Harassment can take many forms: bullying, isolation, rudeness and denigration, or discrimination. Sexual harassment is any kind of unwanted sexual advance or behaviour that is sexual in tone or undertone and is unacceptable in a professional environment. Neither, of course, is restricted to women.

If you experience any form of harassment and feel strong enough, the best course of action is to confront the perpetrator immediately and firmly tell them to stop such behaviour. Very few people are able to do this, however, usually because the aggressors choose their victims for their vulnerability, either due to their temperament or to their position, so it is often those younger or newer employees who are targeted. Harassment of any kind is particularly insidious when perpetrated by someone in authority because it leaves the victim feeling she has no safe place to turn. If you experience this repugnant behaviour as a new employee, you may fear there is nothing you can do about the situation without endangering your career, which is exactly what the perpetrator is relying on. The situation is particularly distressing as the victim often feels guilty, even though there is no rational reason why she should; this is also the reason why many such incidents are not addressed. If you ever find yourself in such a situation, I do encourage you to find the courage to speak up to put a stop to it.

If someone makes you feel uncomfortable by an inappropriate remark or gesture, try to make clear how it makes you feel and set boundaries immediately. Say something like: 'That makes me feel uncomfortable; you have overstepped a boundary from work; I hope that will never happen again'. This often works; simply by calling the inappropriate behaviour out, the perpetrator realises they must stop.

Make a note of what happened and when. This will not be easy, because you just want to forget the unpleasant episode, but it is necessary if you are to deal with the problem. If you weren't able to speak to the aggressor, try writing to them, which also documents that the behaviour is unwanted and unacceptable and must stop.

Another often helpful strategy is to get help from a colleague who can provide informal support – and that may be the end of the matter. One instance of this took place in a law firm where one of the female interns was being sexually harassed by a junior associate. She asked for help from another (male) junior associate who went to her aid and told his colleague to back off. That settled the matter there but of course may not have prevented the behaviour continuing somewhere else, and for this reason, organisations have codes of conduct and guidelines about sexual harassment which they try to enforce. Where possible, you should always try to go down the formal route.

Aggressors are more likely to be called out on their behaviour since the #MeToo movement, and so in the interests of stopping harassment victims are called upon to report it. Find out to whom unprofessional behaviour of this kind should be reported in your firm; it could be HR or a specialised office such as an ethics office. There may be a staff counsellor to whom you can turn for advice and support, but that is not the same as reporting the incident.

As a young woman, you may feel it is beyond your strength to fight this battle, especially, of course, if your manager is harassing you, so there may be no other alternative than finding a new place of employment. It is important that you leave with your integrity intact, but make sure to inform HR why you are leaving.

For your journal

1. Read up your organisation's harassment and sexual harassment policies.
2. Be prepared to rebuff any unwanted and unacceptable behaviour.
3. Be ready to offer your support to a colleague who becomes the victim of harassment or sexual harassment with advice and practical help.

GETTING SUPPORT

None of us can get along without support. You cannot work on your career development or make a successful career transition without investing time and effort in building up a mutual support network which will help you do your current job better and also prepare the ground to achieve your ambitions.

Support groups are everywhere: seek out colleagues who have advanced in their career in the organisation and ask them how they did it. If there is no peer group or internal women's support or mentoring network at your organisation, why not create one, together with like-minded colleagues? In a large organisation, this can be done across departments or even locations; but even if you work in a small or medium-sized enterprise (SME), there are opportunities enough; you just have to create them by reaching out to people who can support you. There is a great advantage in being part of such a group within your company as you will be more visible and can lobby for your interests and for support such as coaching or training. Get your HR department on board. Some companies have internal career coaches to help their employees progress, and even if yours doesn't, you can ask if there's a budget for an external career coach. And of course, check out the talent development programmes that your company offers, where you will find a ready-made support network of people like yourself.

DOI: 10.4324/9781003353720-15

Most organisations require managers to take an active role in nurturing talented employees and to hold regular career conversations to discuss your career aspirations and identify together where you can create opportunities for growth and development. This can happen through skills training, special assignments, being lent to a different department to get an additional perspective, or by opportunities to get more exposure such as representing the department at a meeting or giving a presentation to an internal or external audience.

Go well prepared to these career conversations and have ready ideas and suggestions for development activities. Make it clear in which direction you would like to go – you are aiming for the next step on the career ladder and want to make strategic steps in your present organisation. At the same time, the meeting is also an opportunity to get feedback from your manager on how they see you. This important reality check will open your eyes to any gaps you need to close.

Your manager can be an important ally in your career development as they know how the organisation works and can be instrumental in getting you the right assignments and opportunities, which will, in turn, enable you to move onwards and upwards.

BUILDING AND NURTURING YOUR NETWORK

Your network is quite literally one of your most valuable resources: a fantastic pool of people you can turn to for various kinds of help and support in your professional development. You will already be using social networks such as Facebook, Twitter, LinkedIn, etc. But do you use them strategically? And don't overlook contacts such as:

1. family, family friends, and acquaintances
2. the community of university alumni
3. your friends (present and past)
4. contacts from social activities such as the gym or your dance class
5. people you meet socially

6. work colleagues including HR
7. professional contacts through work
8. contacts from training courses and meetings
9. contacts from conferences and events organised by professional associations
10. career development professionals such as a career coach
11. other professionals, e.g. lawyer, accountant.

Your network will be important throughout your career development for different reasons, but it is invaluable at a time of transition, when you need to reach out to people who can give you information about the kind of work you are interested in, industry updates, the best organisations, referrals, recommendations, etc. You can spread your network as wide as you like but it's also really useful to create a strong network of support within your own organisation.

Case study

Felicia, a junior solicitor, felt her talent was not appreciated by her line manager who consistently refused to give her the kind of tasks that she felt she was more than capable of. She had formed a very useful network in her law firm by being the focal point for the women lawyers in the firm, which gave her excellent visibility and also allowed her to get to know senior lawyers. Through her network, she learned that a colleague was leaving the firm. Felicia knew this colleague's manager was supportive of women's career development and open to new ideas and so she approached him to ask if she could apply for the position. Because she had taken the initiative and was well-known thanks to her work as a focal point, she stood out from the group of potential applicants and the manager encouraged her to apply. She got the job, which she would not even have known about without her network.

What role can your contacts play? Supporters, mentors, sponsors, information-givers, door-openers. I recounted my own experience in the preface when, with the help of one person who opened that first door, I was able to make the transition to a new career. There were many other people in my network: friends who gave moral support (and one friend who even offered financial support); people who gave advice and provided information about qualifications and formalities. It pays to put the effort into broadening your network of contacts as you never know how they might be able to help you further on in your career – or indeed how you might, in turn, be able to be of service to them.

In no career transition is support more important than when you go independent. This is the moment when you realise how different kinds of contacts in your network can play a role in your new life; not only the people in your profession but also those who have experience of self-employment and other professionals such as tax experts whom you will now need.

When you create your networking map in your journal (see below), do it with a new self-employed hat on.

Case study

Diane from the publishing industry emphasised that she had a good network of contacts in the form of ex-colleagues who helped her in terms of giving recommendations to new clients, which started her off with a client base. She also joined a freelance hot-desking group, initially just to get out of the house and have somewhere different to work and hold meetings, but she found that this space quickly became much more than that as she connected with other freelancers and was able to swap stories, get advice, and share different approaches to freelancing. In effect, this was a support group. In terms of the more technical aspects of setting up on her own, Diane sought out help from the start. Money and finance management were an aspect that she knew she needed help with, so she asked for recommendations for an accountant. And she also spoke to other freelancers about setting up a website. By getting support in all the peripheral (but essential) areas, Diane was able to concentrate her energy on what she was best at – the core elements of publishing.

For your journal

1. Create a map of your network with yourself in the middle with contacts around you.
2. Reflect on what support you need at the moment – is it information, advice, suggestions, contacts,…?

3. Identify the contacts who could provide what you need. If you see gaps in your network map that need filling, make a note of how you could potentially fill them.
4. Ask the people in your network map if they can put you in touch with anyone who can give you the kind of information/advice you are looking for.
5. Use your social networks and professional and alumni associations to search for the right person.
6. Revisit your network map regularly to add new contacts.
7. When you have a professional conversation with someone, always ask if they can recommend someone else to whom you could talk. Make your network grow effectively!

Notice that you are not necessarily asking anyone for a job. You are simply using your network to gather information on a regular and ad hoc basis. At the same time, you are strengthening the bonds of your network and signalling that you are there for others, too, when they need you. Networking is a two-way activity.

GETTING BACK IN TOUCH

Returning to the employed working space after a break, possibly of some years, requires special support of all kinds: first from your family to reassure you that they are going to be all right and then from your network to actually find the best place to take up your professional life again. We saw how Lorna and Pamela managed their return in Part 1, but here I would like to look particularly at the use of support networks. Frequently, women lose touch with their professional networks when they take time out of work and find it daunting to pick up those threads. The following stories of Alicia and Noor show that getting support from your network can be a surprisingly positive experience and that, even if it can be disappointing at first, perseverance pays off in the end. The two stories demonstrate the value of building a network with different kinds of contacts.

Case study

Alicia had a Bachelor's degree in Economics and an MBA and had worked in banking for a couple of years after leaving university, but gave up her professional career when she had her two daughters and subsequently devoted herself to being a wife, mother, and homemaker. She taught Italian part-time at a private school for a few years, just to do something while her own children were at school, but it was never more than a way of killing a few hours. When her daughters were 16 and 18, Alicia began to feel the urge to return to work in financial services. More specifically, she wanted to work in the field of socially responsible investment banking. She began a chartered accountancy course, in the full knowledge that this would be a challenge.

When faced with putting together her network map, Alicia was adamant that she did not know anyone; she no longer had any professional contacts from the banking world and had lost all contact with anyone from her former life. It was, after all, many years ago. When she reflected more deeply, however, she realised that she did have friends who might know people in the financial services sector and enlisted their help with contacts. She also made an effort to attend events on any topic related to financial services, investment banking, and related topics, and to talk to people there, even if she did not know them.

As a result, she accepted an invitation from her own bank (as a customer) to a talk followed by a drinks reception, where she met two people who were in investment banking, and she was able to follow up with one of them. Slowly but surely, Alicia began to build up her network, which ended up including some people in quite influential positions. She connected with the Johns Hopkins University alumni association and discovered that the CEO of a prestigious private bank was an alumnus. Summoning all her courage, she reached out to him by email. She was astounded when just one week later, his assistant rang to schedule a meeting. He was prepared to give her his time merely on the basis of them both having been to the same university, and at the meeting, he was very helpful with information, tips, and suggestions. He could not offer her a job, but she gained both confidence and concrete information about the sector through meeting him.

Networking is the most effective method for collecting information, opening doors, and creating leads. However, it does not work for everyone to the same degree, and cultural environments can also play a role, as the story of Noor illustrates.

Case study

After her divorce, Noor left California, where she had worked for a commercial real estate developer as a marketing specialist for many years, and returned to the UK, where she was born and where her parents were still living. Noor knew no one in Manchester apart from her parents and a few former school friends. She found the culture alien and the people distant after the open, easy-going way of life in California. She was surprised when she asked people to put her in touch with professional contacts that there was little response. When we worked together, I encouraged Noor to look at ways of widening her network and not restrict herself to personal contacts, which had proved to be a dead-end. She needed to focus on making professional contacts and, as luck would have it, a global corporate real estate conference was scheduled to be held online in just one month's time. For a £150 registration fee, Noor gained admission to a series of interesting keynotes and events which gave her an insight into the current trends and challenges of the industry and – just as important – made some contacts with people who were interested in her knowledge of the California commercial real estate business.

Personal contacts are always a good starting point in your network, but they are not enough. When Noor put herself out there in a professional forum she was pleased to realise that she had a lot to offer and was able to begin to build the professional network she needed.

FINDING A MENTOR

A mentor can provide invaluable support in a career transition, whether it is someone in your organisation or from outside with valuable business experience in the same or a related industry. You can find a mentor outside your company through a mentoring network, which is often adjunct to career networks such as the British Association of Female Entrepreneurs, or Women in Tech. Local, regional, and national women's groups often offer mentor programmes, and many professions have a dedicated women's association, for example, Women in Law and the two mentioned above for female entrepreneurs, which are all ready-made support networks where you can potentially find a mentor.

But your mentor does not have to be a woman. A female mentor can be a plus as a source of inspiration, sharing her experience of dealing with the challenges of being a woman in a frequently male-dominated professional world; but a male mentor will enable you to see things from the male perspective, which can be very valuable. Choose someone you trust and with whom you can be open and honest, who has the relevant experience and is willing to make the time to be available throughout the mentoring relationship. The degree of formality of the mentoring relationship varies. If you become part of a formal mentoring programme, there will be a structured format to the mentoring process, but an informal mentoring relationship can be just as fruitful. A mentoring relationship normally lasts a year and can continue even longer if both parties wish, but a year is the minimum for you to gain a real advantage from the experience.

If you are looking inside your organisation for a mentor, your manager may not be the best choice even if you have a good working relationship with them. Having a mentor in addition to your manager means you are getting advice and support from two sources as opposed to one, as well as a broader business perspective. Your mentor does not even have to be in the same department, but it is important that they know the company well and are willing to give you support to find your feet and navigate the ins and outs of how the company works. Your mentor is someone who can open doors for you.

Many companies have formal mentoring programmes in place for new recruits and high-potential employees and if yours does not, you can ask your HR department or management whether a mentor could be found for you. If you have to do it on your own, look for someone who has a key position from the point of view of knowing how the company works. If you are in a large company, then mid-tier management on the operational side is a good place to look.

The person you select should be someone you can relate to and who you think will be prepared to reserve some time for you and take the mentoring role seriously. In her book *Lean In*, Sheryl Sandberg talks about how her own career path was greatly smoothed by the support of her mentor. She also emphasises that you cannot simply walk into someone's office and ask them to be your mentor. Try to gain access to a working group or some kind of situation where you can begin to form a relationship with the person before you ask them. Ideally, your prospective mentor will have had the opportunity to notice you as someone who is worth mentoring ahead of your request.

A mentor will be extremely helpful if you are transitioning to become independent. Try to find someone with their own business – ideally in the same professional area, but regardless they must have experience as a business owner or consultant.

For your journal

1. Reflect on who could be your mentor and think of ways you can begin to build a relationship with them.
2. Enlist the help of your manager and/or HR to find a suitable mentor within your organisation.
3. Check out the 'Guidelines for a mentoring relationship' in the toolkit provided.

12

MOVING INTO POWER

GAINING EXPERIENCE IN MANAGEMENT SKILLS

It is difficult to become a manager or team lead without having some experience in supervising others. But you can prepare for this transition by looking out for opportunities to learn and practise the management skills of guiding and supervising other people. See if you can mentor or dotted-line manage (i.e. unofficially manage) a more junior or new team member or an intern so that you can gradually build up valuable experience and evidence to show that you are ready to make the transition to management when the time comes.

Most bigger organisations have management training courses; discuss with your manager when you can attend one of these or do some online modules on performance management, goal-setting, or team motivation. In addition, there are many kinds of practical, on-the-job activities you can engage in which will help you acquire the skills needed to transition into becoming a manager, such as:

1. Take an active role in inducting interns, consultants, new team members, etc.
2. Organise an event/meeting/conference.
3. Train and supervise temporary staff such as interns.

DOI: 10.4324/9781003353720-16

4. Chair a meeting.
5. Research a topic of interest, especially something new and cutting-edge in your industry, and then give a presentation to the team on it; become the go-to person on this subject.
6. Establish yourself as an expert for your section in organisational policy.
7. Become a focal point for a substantive area.
8. Become a focal point for a staff group, e.g. gender focal point.
9. Take the lead on a project.
10. Represent your manager when possible.

You can also look for opportunities outside work to develop leadership skills:

1. Become the chairperson of a professional association.
2. Become a member of the steering committee of a voluntary association such as a charity, a local political organisation, or a women's network and chair the group for a year.
3. Organise a charity event.
4. Head up a sports group.
5. Become the president of your university local alumni group.

For your journal

1. Make a list of opportunities available to you to gain managerial skills and experience.
2. Talk to your boss about special assignments that will help you to gain these skills.
3. Research articles and books about management.
4. Attend a management course either in your own organisation or privately.

POWER IN THE SERVICE OF THE TEAM

When you have made the transition to team lead, you are now responsible not only for yourself and your own results but for the results and well-being of your team as well. With responsibility comes power, and how to balance these will be one of your primary concerns as a new manager. Let's look at two women who moved into management roles for the first time, Emma, who outwardly resisted her position of authority and the 'power' she had, and Maya, who was too keen on using it.

Case study

When Emma was appointed as the manager of a group of six in a research institute, she had never managed people before. Well-known in her field and ambitious, her approach was to be 'one of the gang' and not flex her 'power muscle'. She operated an open-door policy, encouraging what she thought was an open, honest environment, introducing 'sharing' opportunities such as a mood wall for everyone to put up comments, articles, photos, ideas, anything they liked. She was the only one who ever put anything on that wall.

Because she was determined to use a hands-off, collegial managerial approach, Emma left her team to get on with their work with very little supervision or guidance. However, she ruthlessly criticised work she considered sub-standard. She soon realised that some of the team were actually not doing as much work as she expected of them and that it was not always of high quality. Emma began to get the feeling that her position was being undermined and that some of her team were actively working against her.

Emma's team did not respond well to her peer-to-peer approach because it ran counter to the truth of the situation, namely that she was the boss, which she made them feel as soon as she noticed work standards slipping. Emma's staff needed guidance from their new manager as well as being able to respect her for her own work ethic. It was up to her to create a productive and harmonious working atmosphere through a sensitive balance of direction, motivation, and support. Sadly, the team felt the discrepancy between her 'friendly' style and how she behaved otherwise. It is not possible to relinquish the responsibility of the managerial position and its attendant power. This is a tightrope act for any new manager, and you can only learn it through great sensitivity and awareness.

On the other hand, when a manager maxes out and abuses her position of power, as in the story of Maya, team motivation and performance inevitably suffer.

Case study

Maya's new position was managing a team of eight in a hotel ban-
queting department, working in two shifts. She came from within the
hospitality industry but had no previous managerial experience. When
she started her new job, she believed she had to show her power and
used a 'divide and rule' approach. She played the morning team off the
afternoon team, comparing their performance in public and generally
cementing a split between them. She would also gather information
and opinions from each team member individually and then repeat in
front of the whole team what she had been told in confidence.

In effect, she abused the trust that her staff had given her by disre-
specting the confidentiality of her one-to-one talks. The result was
a team which was riddled with petty strife, sly manoeuvring, and
one-upmanship. No one trusted anyone else, let alone Maya. It goes
almost without saying that the lack of harmony in the team led to a
lack of motivation and poor performance.

A manager must create cohesion and Maya needed to find
ways to bring her whole team together: in team meetings, keeping constantly in touch with all team members, keeping them all
informed, arranging group events, and if possible, changing the
constellation of the shifts at times to give people a chance to get
to know other colleagues.

The transition to manager is particularly sensitive when you
are promoted from within the team, as in the case of Margaret
who worked in local government.

Case study

Margaret had long been friends with her colleagues Maria and Eva, and
she found it difficult to alter her ways or her attitude towards them
after she had been promoted to team manager. She still had lunch or
coffee regularly with one or both of them, and occasionally would discuss other members of the team with them. She meant no harm, but
the other members of the team resented what they saw as favouritism,
and worried about what was being said about them, which contributed
to a divisive atmosphere.

Margaret faced a challenging situation: she wanted to keep her friendship with Maria and Eva, while at the same time exercising her new authority. When you manage people, you must be aware all the time of how your actions and words are perceived by your staff. You have to be seen to use your position of power fairly. If you are a new manager promoted from within the team talk to your friends, be open about the dilemma and enlist their help and support. Make clear to them that you are sensitive to the responsibilities that your new role brings with it, that you want to avoid the dangers of being perceived as favouring your friends, and that you will not talk about the other team members with them. Hopefully, they will understand, and you will still be able to remain friends.

Many managers (new and seasoned) find it helpful to have a trusted person to whom they can turn in confidence to discuss and resolve issues with their staff. This might be someone within the organisation or it could be an external coach. It is easy to understand how lonely Margaret feels, and how tempting it is for her to continue to use her friends for support, but she must reflect on how this looks and feels to the other staff. Something as simple as having coffee breaks with all your team makes a visible gesture of including everyone so that favouritism does not become an issue.

WHEN TO ASSERT YOUR AUTHORITY

Sometimes it is necessary to exercise your authority energetically, as Joyce found out when she became the manager of a small Learning and Development team and faced a situation where someone in her team tried to undermine her position.

Case study

Joyce's new team of three was divided among themselves with a history of two team members bullying the third. The previous manager had not had any success in solving this problem, which had been happening for some time. The two team members always stuck together, supporting and covering for each other, forming a united side in opposition to their colleague, who often called in sick.

Joyce was determined to tackle the problem and began first to look into the work results. She discovered fairly quickly that the two employees in question were not actually performing as well as they appeared to be. She decided to redistribute areas of work and responsibilities. In retaliation and perhaps to pre-empt being given what they perceived as additional work, one of the two employees in question made a spurious complaint about her. (In fact, he complained that her 7-year-old daughter had spent a few hours in the office. Joyce, a single mother, had been unable to find childcare at short notice when her carer had called in sick and so had brought her daughter to work with her.) That was the last warning signal. Joyce did not hesitate and swiftly arranged for the person to be re-assigned to a different department. She could not allow employees to undermine her authority and she was prepared to use her power to send a strong message to that effect.

Joyce preferred a radical solution to trying to patch over the deep rift in her team. The strategy worked well: the team member who had been bullied revived and took no more sick days; the team member who had been one of the bullies changed her attitude and her performance improved. Sometimes you have to exert your power as a manager in a decisive manner.

Transitioning into power – or more power – requires sensitivity and courage and an understanding of how to use that power. The better you get to know your team, the easier it will be to feel comfortable with being in authority.

For your journal

1. Make a mind map of your team on paper or using small objects on your table to represent each person. Put yourself in the position where you feel you are in relation to them. Looking at the map you have created, reflect on how your team members interact with each other and with you.
2. Consider how you are using the power and authority invested in you as a manager and how your team members are reacting.

3. Reflect on whether there is tension within the team and what you can do to alleviate that tension by using your power wisely.

SHOWING EMPATHY

As you settle into your role as a manager, always see the members of your team as people and draw on your capacity for caring when you work with them. People's behaviour can sometimes be baffling, and when their behaviour starts affecting their work or the team, your empathy mode needs to kick in. There is always a reason for the way people behave even if it is not clear to you at first, and simply remembering this and showing that you care will go a long way to creating a positive working relationship between you and your team.

The experience of living through the Covid-19 pandemic has shown us how vulnerable we are in our mental health and just how badly sickness and the deaths of family members and people we know can affect us. Managers have had to deal with issues that they may never have thought they would face. I was coaching a seasoned manager who, when about to transition to a new role in the same organisation, let out a heartfelt cry: 'I'm not a psychologist!'; voicing the helplessness that she and many managers have felt in facing the pandemic crisis with their staff. It helps to remember that you are not expected to solve everyone's problems; what you can do is listen and express your concern. By simply taking the time to listen and be empathetic, you have already played an important part in helping your team member feel better. You can also support your staff by suggesting additional resources for their well-being. Many organisations have well-being teams which offer wellness training, meditation, and counselling. You might also set up small initiatives in your team yourself; the manager I just mentioned organised 'daily instalments' with tips and stories, to which all the team contributed, to help make everyone feel better, and to keep in touch on a personal level, which her team really appreciated. One team I was working with remembered a manager who made a point of checking in at the end of every week with every member of her team and asking,

'What do you need for next week?'. She made each team member feel that she was interested in them, that she heard them and was going to do her best for them. This created a strong team spirit.

Simply by showing you are human makes a huge difference, as Ricarda found out in the following case study.

Case study

Three months into her job as manager of a group of in-house lawyers, Ricarda noticed that one of the administrative assistants, Raoul from Colombia, seemed to have stopped making an effort; he was coming into work later and later and was very often distracted. His output was barely up to the minimum and colleagues had started commenting that they were often held up waiting for him to complete something. Ricarda tried asking him if was unwell but he brushed her off, saying he was fine. She did not want to pry but could not ignore the situation as it was affecting the work of the team.

She asked him to meet her at the company's coffee bar and told him that she was sad to have noticed that his performance had dropped off. She did not ask for an explanation but simply said if there was anything that was troubling him that she could do something about, she would be happy to do it as she valued his work and his presence on the team. Raoul thanked her but said nothing more. Three weeks later, Ricarda received an email from Raoul, thanking her for her offer of help. He told her that his mother was seriously ill in Colombia and he was her only son. He was so worried about his mother that he was incapable of working properly. He was at his wits' end. Ricarda immediately arranged for him to take special leave to go to Colombia.

At first, Raoul had not felt able to open up to Ricarda. She was the boss and in his culture you didn't talk about personal matters to the boss, and especially not as she was a woman.

Problems that team members are experiencing may be due to a whole range of reasons; they may lie in their private life, or in a conflict with someone in the team, or in a new work process with which they are having difficulty, or in any number of other reasons including unconscious ones. Finding out the reason may not be easy and of course, you must respect your staff's privacy, but if you have built up enough trust you may be able to learn the cause of the problem and help solve it. In Raoul's case, Ricarda was patient and sensitive, and she also reached out to him and showed him her human side. Not all team members will open up to you, but by showing you care, as Ricarda did, you will leave the door open for them to walk through.

Raoul's case is also a good example of the way in which some people find it difficult to relate to a manager in any context other than a professional one, sometimes especially if the manager is a woman. Cultural backgrounds often play a role here. It takes time and a sensitive approach to build up a trusting, professional relationship, and you can make a big difference by allowing your team to see you as a human being who is interested in them as people.

We all have parts of ourselves that we show to the world, others we show only to our family or close friends, and some that are hidden even to ourselves.

Ask yourself how you could share a little more about yourself than you are perhaps doing. The more your team is able to perceive you as a fully rounded person and not only in the box of 'the manager', or 'authority', the more they will feel able to trust you, which in turn will lead to loyalty. Also, note that it is equally as important to share information with your team about things in the department and the organisation as a whole that affect them. Your staff will appreciate your being open and transparent.

People are at work for different reasons: some may be interested in the job they are doing; a few may actually love it; some, perhaps even the majority, may see their work simply as a means to an end, to earn enough money to live. You need to get close enough to each member of your team to know what motivates them and also what concerns them, and when you show interest and understanding you have already taken a step towards getting them on your side.

Each member of the team is also a complete person, with a life outside the office, with their own worries and hopes. Each has their own past that has shaped them. If you can see the whole person and not just their role at work, you will learn how to support them to perform better and will strengthen their loyalty to you. The aim is to strike the right balance between empathy and distance – a case of compassionate detachment in which you express interest and compassion towards the employee but retain the necessary objective detachment and authority.

When giving constructive feedback, do not allow yourself to be preoccupied by feelings of empathy as you will fear giving feedback and will not be able to carry through. Rather, you should be pragmatic about what is best for your team and your company. If you shy away from confrontation, it is not easy to regain ground; you must not allow employees to exploit your goodwill, just as you may not abuse your position of power. If you can develop a way of being which combines a fundamental belief in your staff's desire to cooperate and do their best with a detached objectivity, you will be able to stand firm when necessary. Help your staff to look for solutions to problems, but acknowledge the problem as being theirs, for which they must accept both the responsibility and the consequences.

Jacqueline arrived as a new manager leading the market research team at a manufacturing support company. Quite quickly, it became clear to her that her executive assistant, Helen, was not performing up to standard.

Case study

Helen had worked at the company for many years, and Jacqueline was hoping she could rely on Helen's experience and company know-how to help her in her transition, but found the reality was far from this. Helen often missed deadlines, made mistakes, forgot to schedule important meetings, and called in sick frequently. This was not the support that Jacqueline needed. She attempted more than once to address the problem, and although there was some brief improvement, Helen then quickly lapsed back into not pulling her weight.

Jacqueline decided enough was enough and one day called Helen into her office to tell her that things could not go on like this and that Helen's job was on the line, at which Helen burst into tears. She tried to put the blame on others in the team, adding that her previous manager had always appreciated her work and never criticised her. Jacqueline's instinctive reaction was to sympathise and back down, but she realised that would harm her position as a manager. She stood her ground and kept silent. She knew that she must not lose her authority. She also knew she was in the right and was determined to help Helen accept responsibility for herself.

Helen finally admitted her slack attitude and explained she was feeling overwhelmed by policy and procedure changes that had been introduced in the company and was unsure of herself. This was the breakthrough Jacqueline had been waiting for. Together they drew up a plan to help Helen find her feet again.

Jacqueline struggled with her natural tendency to be empathetic but realised that in this case, the right solution was decisiveness, not empathy.

For your journal

1. Reflect on the personalities of the members of your team and their behaviour and consider how you can support each of them to do their best.
2. Reflect on how empathetic you are and where you think you may need to be more empathetic.
3. Consider where you can refer your staff to professionals for help and support if necessary.
4. Reflect on how open you are and think about how you could share more with your team.

WHICH MANAGEMENT STYLE?

You may find yourself faced with one dilemma specific to women: whether to adopt a directional and results-oriented style and run the risk of being perceived as distant and lacking in empathy or whether to retain traits that could be considered feminine, such as sensitivity, empathy, inclusiveness, and a talent for compromise, which may lead to you being perceived as weak and indecisive.

Case study

Nina was appointed as head of a specialist design team in an engineering company with a predominantly male workforce, and indeed, her team of five were all men. She believed that she had to pre-empt any resentment at her being a woman and should show that she was tough and ready to take on all challenges. So, she favoured a transactional leadership style: she was uncompromising, took decisions without consulting anyone in her team, and micro-managed everyone. Her (highly competent) team was stunned and within a few months, some were thinking of leaving.

It is true that sometimes there is latent resentment that may consciously or unconsciously exist towards women managers, and this is more prevalent in some industries and cultures than others. Antje, a Dutch chemical engineer who worked for a global energy corporation, told me: 'I always had to prove myself before the male colleagues would accept me as their manager, but as soon as they realised I was fully up to speed on the work there was no problem. When you demonstrate excellent technical knowledge, colleagues are always willing to accept your authority.' However, it is best not to go into a role assuming that there will be resentment towards you as a woman manager. This is where Nina went wrong – she made an assumption before she had actually established what her team were like and how they would react to her.

It would have been better if Nina had approached her new role by first establishing her credentials and earning the respect of her team members and then gaining their trust by listening to them and learning about their successes and their concerns. This would not have been hard to do and would have enabled her to exercise true authority based on her expertise.

Rather than worrying about which management style to adopt, concentrate rather on which attributes are effective and what feels right for your particular context.

For your journal

Consider the following table and reflect on your own behaviour.

Attribute	*Behaviour*
Authority and credibility	I give clear directions, demonstrate expertise, and lead by example
Good judgement and follow-through	I make difficult decisions and stand by them
Transparent decision-making	I include my team in decision-making processes where possible and always keep my team informed

(Table continued)

Attribute	Behaviour
Empathy	I listen to others, put myself in their shoes before commenting or making a decision, and try where possible to take individual wishes into consideration
Fairness	I am inclusive and do not tolerate discrimination; I evaluate impartially
Expertise	I am an expert in my field, keep up to date with latest developments, and share my knowledge with my team
Develop staff	I conduct career development discussions regularly and support the career aspirations of my team members
Create team spirit	I check in with individual team members regularly; I communicate a sense of purpose and identity

THE ART OF DELEGATION

When you become a manager or transition to leading a bigger team, it may seem that your time simply evaporates, and even when you leave the office, you feel you have so much to do that you cannot relax – you begin to work at all hours to keep on top of it all.

You may feel unprepared for the new demands on your time throughout the day: planning and organising the team's work, budgeting, reporting upwards, distributing and monitoring tasks and results, dealing with clients and partners, and above all managing the people who make up your team, and in addition you are supposed to do your 'own work'.

This load may leave you feeling physically drained and mentally overwhelmed. How to cope with it all? How to fulfil the expectations which have been placed on you and perform in the stellar manner which has been your trademark up to now? In the transition from team member to team lead or when you have transitioned to leading a bigger team, it is vital to pace yourself and learn to cope strategically with the new position and the plethora of demands that are being made on you. Accept that you cannot be all things to all people; accept that you cannot do everything yourself. Learn to delegate. Learn to say 'no' when necessary. Recognise what tasks are redundant.

You may find it hard to stop yourself doing everything that needs to be done. This is one of your cardinal challenges because so far in your career, you have usually carried out your tasks on your own, with some input from the rest of the team. Now, it is up to you to plan the work of the team, including your own work. Your main responsibility is to *manage*, not *do* the work of the team. Delegating means trusting your team to do their work. It means creating a positive working environment and then letting go and empowering them, which is actually motivating to everyone involved. Only by doing this will you free yourself up to meet the more strategic, leadership elements of your role and, equally important, to fulfil your own work objectives without hitting burnout.

During the pandemic, the art of delegation became even more difficult when teams were working remotely, and managers had to find ways of keeping track of tasks in a virtual space while also being aware of and mitigating the huge challenges that many employees were facing working from home. As we move into the phase of hybrid working in one form or another, leaders will be called upon to design methods for delegating fairly and monitoring their team's progress while of course continuing to keep everyone together.

For your journal

1. What can only I do?
2. Which part of my responsibilities can be delegated and to whom?
3. Which tasks are redundant?
4. Do I make enough time for the strategic, leadership elements of my role?

INSPIRING YOUR TEAM

Even as a junior manager, you have the chance to make an impact on other people and inspire them to be the best in their jobs. You can be the leader they want to follow. Begin by making a list of the things that you believe are important for a strong team that works well together and produces good results. Examples of things you might have on your list are: inclusiveness; innovation; team spirit and mutual support; willingness to learn; equality and fairness; transparent decision-making; opportunities for career development; the desire to produce good work; and a caring attitude.

When you have your list, ask yourself how you can be a role model for these things and what you could introduce to make them happen. Then, when you have some ideas for yourself, invite your team to take part in the process of creating the working atmosphere that they feel would be most productive. Have a brown bag lunch session to create a mood board of ideas; let everyone have their say. Find out what is important for your team and inspire in them a sense of being able to achieve great results together.

Case study

When Roxanna took over as head of a fundraising section for a global charity six years ago, her team consisted of two employees, but as a direct result of the pandemic in 2020 demand for funds and supplies grew and suddenly she had to hire four new employees. In the midst of the crisis, she had to on-board, train, and integrate her new team members into the business. She says her main priority was to inspire them as she believed that would lead to them doing their best and producing the required results. In order to do this, she drew on what inspired her the most in her role – the organisation's mission of helping children in need. Roxana brought her team back to this goal again and again. In addition, she inspired her team by giving them areas of specific responsibility so that they felt they were integral to the success of each project. She also acted as a role model with a strong work ethic, demonstrating dedication and commitment to work and yet balancing that with a fulfilled private life.

It is also worth stopping to consider who inspires you. Who are your role models? These can be public figures, women in the same industry as you, teachers from your school or college days, women from your own family, or wider circle of friends. How do they behave? How did they achieve what they did? What makes them special and how can you emulate that? It can be both inspiring and comforting to think of these women who went before you and led the way, now beckoning you to follow in their footsteps by being the best you can be.

For your journal

1. Reflect on who has inspired you in your life and make notes about what makes them inspiring.
2. How might you apply some of these characteristics to inspire yourself?
3. How will you inspire others?

13

PLANNING YOUR FUTURE CAREER DEVELOPMENT

Where do you see yourself in five years and who and what will help you get there? To achieve your ambitions, you must plan your career moves strategically.

Planning your further career steps is a skill in itself, one that you need to develop and practise continuously using the guidelines and tips in this book.

It is useful to assess how much support your organisation offers for the career transition into and career development within it. What does the organisation's talent management look like? Consider the opportunities for growth and development within the organisation and whether they will invest in your career through training, mentoring, and career coaching. Is there a clear message from HR and senior management that women are actively supported in their career aspirations? Take a look at whether they offer mentoring, talent groups for women, and internal training. Many companies have excellent diversity programmes where they proactively support specific groups including women, ethnic minorities, and LGBTQ+ employees in their career paths.

There are several people who can be a great help to you in your strategic career planning, not least your line manager, so schedule and plan a career discussion with them. Together create your development goals both for the coming year and for the

DOI: 10.4324/9781003353720-17

longer term and then identify learning opportunities where you can develop your skills and knowledge to match those goals. Be especially alert to ways in which you can gain experience in operational areas that have a major role to play in the company. Challenge yourself not only to build on what you already know and can do but also be prepared to learn new skills and gain knowledge in new areas. This is also how you become visible to senior people in your organisation as a colleague with high potential.

Discuss with your manager how you could take on extra responsibility for new tasks, areas, and projects and how you can gain experience in a supervisory or managerial role, as this can be a Catch-22 situation – it's hard to become a manager without managerial experience, but how do you first get the experience?! To enable you to prepare for this move (or perhaps more importantly illustrate your readiness for it), seek out opportunities to learn how to manage others. The chapter 'Moving into power' looks at this in detail. Support from your line manager is key to putting in place the right measures for career progression, but you are the one who has to do most of the heavy lifting; you must have an idea of where you want to go in order to have effective career conversations with them.

For your journal

Check out the activity 'How to Gain a Good Reputation and Get Yourself Noticed' in the toolkit.

Take the time to do some strategic planning when you are thinking of a career move, when you have bagged a new position and are about to move and are in between career transitions, take stock of the progress you have made and what needs to be done next.

Case study

When Stephanie moved from being Chief of Section in the country office of a humanitarian organisation to a position which gave her a greater scope of activity as Deputy Chief of Section in a regional headquarters, she was keen to make the most of this career transition. In her previous position, she had run an office of six staff members with additional support from consultants. Now, she was part of a much bigger operation at a regional level, responsible for her own team of 12 with responsibility for coordinating the programmes of 14 countries belonging to a huge and very diverse region. It is always a challenge in any organisation to move from a country-focused role to a regional one, and the job was certainly going to be a steep learning curve. But Stephanie was ready for it. She was also determined that this position would be her stepping-stone to her next career transition, namely, to be a Country Representative, i.e. the head of her organisation's operations in a country.

She wasted no time and well ahead of her arrival in the new posting she began to plan meticulously what areas she would need to learn more about, which people she wanted to include in her network, and how she would increase her visibility. Stephanie was fortunate in having a great ally in her new boss, a female leader who fully realised the importance of attending to one's career progression; she encouraged Stephanie to think strategically and offered her support with opening doors to key opportunities.

For your journal

1. Take stock of where you are in your career and reflect on where you would like to be in 5 or 10 years. You can do this as a kind of visualisation; try to see yourself in the position you would like.
2. Begin to plan the steps needed to progress towards your long-term career goal and reflect on what you need to learn or experience in order to get there. Make a learning and development plan.
3. Identify people who could help you and consider how you can make them aware of your talents.
4. Reflect on the challenges you may face and how you will meet those.
5. Reflect on and identify opportunities to stretch yourself and do something a little out of your comfort zone that will help you gain the extra experience you need.

REFLECTION

Mastering these skills is like entering an unknown landscape and deciding that you're going to be observant about your path and make conscious decisions about which turn to take, instead of wandering aimlessly and hoping to find your way. In this way, you get a feeling for the place and begin to feel at home in it. You start to notice patterns and landmarks that you can use as signposts. You become sensitive to changes in the atmosphere, the weather, the light, and the wind. Perhaps you have a map which will help you find your way, but even the best maps are only two-dimensional approximations of the terrain, so you have to use your senses and your wits and draw your own conclusions as to the best route. It is an adventure, and sometimes we take a wrong turn. The main thing is to learn from our missteps and start off again confidently.

PART IV

BELIEVING IN YOURSELF

14

AIMING FOR SATISFACTION IN YOUR CAREER JOURNEY

Being yourself and believing in who you are is essential when it comes to your career journey and the realisation of your aspirations and dreams. Do not be afraid to embrace who you are and aim for what you want. Remember that your personality, your talents, and your worldview are all unique and have much to offer the world – and the workplace.

Every woman can shape who she is; you are not bound by your past and for this reason, a career transition is a key moment in your life as it is a time when you can make a fresh start and step into who you want to be.

FINDING SELF-CONFIDENCE – THE CONCEPT OF BEING GOOD ENOUGH

Many of us are aware of the famous Michelle Obama quote about being good enough. Every new job, right up to becoming the First Lady of the US, entails a learning curve. You cannot know everything from Day 1, but it helps to have the growth mindset along with the confidence that you will be able to learn fast and succeed in your new job.

Yet many women – even successful ones – lack self-confidence. Do you remember Lorna from Part 1, who had a Master's degree in Environmental Science from Heidelberg University and an MBA from Harvard? She was on a teaching fellowship at Harvard when her husband, Robert, was offered a senior management job in a national energy company in his home country in Europe which they both felt he could not turn down. So, they moved with their two small children to the capital city of the European country in which Robert had grown up.

Case study

Lorna admitted, with a gentle laugh, that she was worried she 'wasn't good enough' when she began to think about where she could find a professional setting for herself. With gold-star academic qualifications and a track record in one of the most urgently needed and dynamic fields of our time, she nevertheless lacked the confidence to go out and take the steps necessary to find a suitable new position.

Several factors contributed to Lorna's paralysis: feeling out of place in a new country and a sense of having lost her value, but the lack of confidence in herself is striking. She allowed herself to believe that she was not 'good enough' and questioned her own abilities.

Lorna and I had several months of coaching together during which she built up her self-confidence enough to begin to reach out to people in her network to get meetings with senior managers in potential companies, gathering information and letting people know she was looking for a job – this finally led to her being offered a position to set up a new sustainability programme in a transport network.

It would appear that many women (not all!) only apply for a job when they believe they meet 100% of the qualifications – and more! By contrast, many men will apply even if they only meet 60%. Their self-confidence allows them to persuade themselves that 60% is good enough and that the remaining 40% is something they will soon get the hang of – and that self-confidence often gets them the job as well. There are several reasons why women don't apply for a particular job, including the fact that they may set the bar lower and only apply if they truly meet all the requirements. I have coached many women in applying successfully for positions which they were initially hesitant to apply for as they did not match exactly the stated requirements. Research done by The Behavioural Insights Team on recruitment via LinkedIn supports the view that women believe in the literal terms of a job advert. It is probably a mixture of belief in the system and in some cases a lack of confidence that one could overcome the system that lies at the root of the issue.

The equation is simple: more men than women apply for the job, and of those who apply the men are more persuasive at interview, so more men than women get the jobs, as a rule. The kind of self-confidence that these men possess is sometimes perceived as 'over-confidence', but it is not mere bluster. People who really believe in themselves and in their ability to learn fast actually do a good job. They are not trying to deceive anyone. It is this kind of confidence that we women need to boost in ourselves – the realisation that we are definitely good enough, which will carry us through to acting upon that self-confidence.

In our coaching sessions, we did not spend much time analysing why Lorna had lost her self-confidence but instead focused on looking to the future. Lorna reminded herself of her achievements and her many strengths in addition to her qualifications; she identified situations in the past where she had been able to convince others of her point of view; she put herself in situations a little bit out of her comfort zone, practising assertiveness and poise, and gradually she re-gained the self-confidence that she had lost.

AVOIDING THE PERFECTIONIST TRAP

Throughout this book, I emphasise how important I believe it is to always aim to do the best you can. But we must also accept that there are times when we will not achieve as highly as we had hoped, or that 'done' is better than 'perfect'. Perfectionists are vulnerable during a career transition because there are two kinds of traps that they can fall into: either they put themselves under huge stress to perform well in their new job and are then completely devastated if they don't reach the high standard they have set themselves or they are so afraid of failure that they may exclude themselves from challenges to make sure they don't fail, which leads to missed opportunities and increases overall stress.

A useful strategy against perfectionism is to see the overall cause or objective of your work as bigger than you are. That way you are more prepared to put yourself out there in the interests of achieving a higher cause as you are only part of the picture and you can't be held responsible for the whole thing. Also, if you wait until you are perfect (!), you are preventing the wider world from benefitting from your skills and unique perspective on the world or a particular problem.

If you are a perfectionist, you will find the concept of 'good enough' or 'done is better than perfect' helpful, even if you don't necessarily fully buy in to this at first.

For your journal

I am good enough

1. Consider the career transition you have in mind and write down what would be necessary to make that transition.
2. When you have your list, take a good look at everything and tick off every point where you know you have the skills and qualities required or what you believe you could handle with some learning time.
3. How many points have you ticked? More than half? Three quarters? Nearly everything? As long as you have ticked the majority of points, you are good enough. Let that thought sink in.

I am good enough and do not need to be perfect

1. Write down one of your current goals or projects and define what success will look like when you have finished.
2. Adjust the success criteria to represent what you could accept as good enough but not perfect.

3. When you have accomplished this, accept it as your success.

Striving to do the best you can is a constructive attitude; striving to be perfect in everything, on the other hand, can actually be destructive because you fail to put things into perspective. We will now look at some techniques to help counter this tendency.

For your journal

Getting positive feedback

1. Ask 5–6 people, preferably a mix of friends and colleagues, to give you positive feedback by making brief notes on 2–3 situations when you showed special competence in something. Ask them to identify the skills or abilities you demonstrated.
2. Go back to your success stories and strengths that you listed in Part 1 and compare the strengths that others identified with the ones you see in yourself. Are they different or the same? Are there additional strengths you had not thought of?

Recognising my achievements

1. Make a list of your key achievements in life – this could be gaining qualifications, success in a job role, positive feedback from friends or colleagues, contributions to your local community or charities, or perhaps progress with a hobby.
2. Be quite specific about what makes that event an achievement and pinpoint your abilities and talents that helped you achieve what you did.
3. Take a moment to reflect on and honour your achievements and the talents that underpin them.

15

PRACTISING BEING WHO YOU ARE

APPEARING CONFIDENT

When we are comfortable with ourselves, we behave in a way congruent with who we are. However, there are nuances to our identity: who we are at work is different from who we are at home; we naturally adapt our behaviour slightly towards colleagues (again, with variations) compared to our behaviour towards our family or our friends. Some of this adaptation is related to our desire or need to fit in to the context in which we find ourselves. Most of us feel more comfortable not sticking out like a sore thumb but try to use our sense antennae to pick up signals from our environment to be accepted by our co-habitants and co-workers. This adaptation process calls upon us to dance between our fundamental identity and how much we feel the need to behave in a manner appropriate to the social context.

Case study

Mary-Jo is second generation Chinese-American from a fairly traditional Chinese family background, living in Northern California. She was an exceptionally bright child at school and went on to study software engineering at the University of California Berkeley. After graduating,

DOI: 10.4324/9781003353720-20

she was snapped up by a top tech firm in Silicon Valley and rose steadily in corporate hierarchy as she moved from one firm to the next.

When I met her she was still only 29 and in charge of a team of 18 software engineers, most of whom were men. She came for coaching because, as she put it, 'no one takes me seriously'. This seemed hard to believe, given the fact that she had a very responsible position and that she and her team consistently delivered the required results.

What came to light in our conversation was that although her staff did end up following her directions and performed well, in day-to-day interactions she felt that they treated her 'like a little sister'.

It is true that in Silicon Valley, the collegial tone is informal and there is a flat hierarchy. Mary-Jo was comfortable with this but nevertheless was bothered by the way her staff treated her.

Mary-Jo is all of 5 ft 2 ins and has her hair cut in a short bob. She dresses in a casual style, as befits a tech company in Silicon Valley, usually wearing sneakers with jeans and a sparkly T-shirt. She hadn't seen any need to change her style of dressing since high school. She looks, in fact, like the archetypal little sister. When I suggested that she consider adapting her appearance to fit her managerial role she was taken aback and rejected the idea, saying that wouldn't be her.

After probing, Mary-Jo admitted there was a conflict between how she perceived herself and how others perceived her as she presented herself in a manner more suited to an identity which had been almost imposed upon her as she grew up. As the youngest child and only daughter in a family with four sons, she had always been treated to some extent as the baby of the family. Her parents and brothers all adored her but had been a little uncomfortable with her increasingly sharp intelligence. Partly to appease them, she had assumed a non-threatening persona in her outward appearance, knowing full well that she outdid them in intellectual achievements. This had now become second nature, and even as she grew older, she automatically reached for the same kind of clothes, had her hair cut in the same way, and continued to eschew makeup.

We explored how she might make minimal changes, such as adding a blazer to her jeans and t-shirt outfit, without compromising on her style. Within a few weeks, she returned and the expression on her face was almost smug: it had worked. Her team had changed their casually playful attitude towards her; they listened more respectfully and teased her less. She was adamant that she had not changed anything else. How did she feel now? 'More grown up; more me,' she said thoughtfully, 'I can't believe what a difference it has made.'

Mary-Jo had adapted her behaviour to her work context. She had also very slightly adapted her appearance to reflect better who she was. She was one persona, inside and outside: young and hip, but also a highly professional manager. No one felt inclined to treat her like their little sister.

BEATING IMPOSTOR SYNDROME

People who suffer from impostor syndrome (or phenomenon as it is sometimes called) feel that they are actually not as competent as they appear and are not really able to do their job well; they live in constant fear of being found out as incompetent despite the facts which show they are often excellent at their job. In a career transition, this can be a huge challenge because it may prevent them from applying for positions or from accepting a position they are offered. They carry the burden of feeling inadequate around all the time.

If you suffer from impostor syndrome, you are not alone. A study of 1,000 UK adults conducted by The Hub Events found that a stunning 90% of the women surveyed admitted to feeling inadequate or incompetent at work and 73% didn't feel they deserved their current success! Of these, 17% said that they experience these feelings often or all of the time. Over half the women admitted to experiencing the kind of intrusive thoughts that are associated with impostor syndrome: believing that they don't deserve their position, that it was only due to luck that they have achieved success, that they only got the job or promotion because there weren't enough candidates, and so on.

Anyone can suffer from impostor syndrome, including celebrities who have spoken out about it. Sheryl Sandberg, Chief Operating Officer of Facebook and author of *Lean In*, for example, famously said 'every time I didn't embarrass myself—or even excelled–I believed that I had fooled everyone yet again. One day soon, the jig would be up.'

And Arianna Huffington, co-founder of *The Huffington Post*, founder and CEO of Thrive Global, and author of 15 books:

> The greatest obstacle for me has been the voice in my head that I call my obnoxious roommate. […] we should realize how important it is to stop this negative self-talk. It means pushing back against our obnoxious roommate with a dose of wisdom.

People who suffer from impostor syndrome often attribute their success to outside factors ('it was a team effort', 'I just got lucky'). This is exactly how Melinda felt:

Case study

Melinda joined the civil service straight out of university, where she had studied languages and history, and progressed steadily in her career there. When a post as head of a training department became vacant, the division head encouraged Melinda to apply but at first she refused. 'I thought I'd just been lucky to get as far as I had. There were some really clever people around. We had to take an exam as part of the recruitment process for that post' she recalls, and the man who had been deputy until then also sat for it, but I got the higher marks. I actually thought he would be the right one for the post, but the division head chose me. I was terrified. The responsibility for so many people and all the work was overwhelming. I felt almost as though I had got the job fraudulently. I didn't feel I deserved it. I seriously doubted whether I could deliver what was expected of me.

There's the tell-tale impostor syndrome phrase here: '*I felt almost as though I had got the job fraudulently.*' There was no doubt that Melinda was capable of doing the job of department head in anybody's mind but her own. She admits now that she has been very successful in her new role, but she remembers vividly her lack of self-confidence and feeling not up to the job at the beginning.

If you suffer from impostor syndrome, positive affirmations can be a very useful tool in overcoming negative self-talk. By replacing negative thoughts (that little voice in your head) with positive ones they can have a startling effect.

An affirmation is a short phrase that you choose as your motto for the day. Practise your affirmations daily so that the brain gets used to the new way of thinking. By repeating the affirmation several times, you override the negative thoughts and retrain your way of thinking so that you have more positive patterns of thought. Here are some affirmations to try.

Affirmations

You can also find these affirmations in your toolkit.

1. I am grounded and confident
2. I am aware of my abilities
3. I meet the day's challenges in a positive way
4. There are no blocks that I can't overcome
5. I am worthy of having what I want
6. I can achieve whatever I want
7. All I need is within me
8. I release anything that does not serve me
9. I draw on my strengths
10. Everything is possible
11. I can do this

For your journal

1. When you hear a voice in your head saying you are not able to do something, stop and say out loud 'Yes I can!'
2. Take 10 minutes every week to reflect on what you have achieved.
3. Choose an affirmation every morning and repeat it several times during the day.

BEING RESILIENT

As a young woman, I expected everything to be plain sailing. I can trace this back to my childhood, as the only child of older parents who worked relentlessly in their unbounded love to clear my path of all potential hazards and problems. Although the attitude of my parents, who only wished for my well-being, is understandable, it did not prepare me well for real life. It is harder to cope with difficulties if we have not learned how to do so early on in life.

You need to develop and increase your resilience (ability to spring back from difficulties) if you are to flourish in career moves. In order to do this, you can prepare for possible challenges so that you are not thrown off balance when they occur and can therefore view them as opportunities to learn and grow.

In a career transition, you will constantly come up against unexpected challenges and obstacles that you did not necessarily foresee, but if you are mentally prepared to accept that these will occur, you are halfway to meeting those challenges and overcoming them.

Professional sportspeople, for example, routinely give themselves handicaps of some kind or another in order to practise for the harder challenge. For example, a famous tennis player was spotted playing a round of golf left-handed, her non-dominant hand. When asked why, she answered: 'to make it harder'.

The left-handed round of golf was a kind of self-test. When you work at overcoming obstacles, sometimes in a planned way, instead of avoiding them, you become more resilient. Situations where you leave your comfort zone on purpose make you more resilient. For example, if speaking in front of an audience is something you do not relish and yet will have to do for your next career step, seek out opportunities to practise. That way, when a bigger challenge appears, you will feel more ready for it and more used to and better at managing the emotions that come with it.

Resilience is made up of four factors, all of which you can strengthen: self-awareness, a sense of purpose, self-care, and good relationships. I would like to add one more: self-forgiveness, which is an ability to walk away when necessary and chalk the failure up to experience. Resilience also means being able to accept a failure and turn the page. Next time, it will be better. Remember that then was then; this is now.

For your journal

1. Consider how resilient you are on a scale of 1–10 where 1 is not resilient at all and 10 is very resilient, where you are able to cope with anything that comes your way. Coping means that you are mentally prepared to say, 'I can overcome this challenge'.
2. Find some examples of when you faced a challenge and remember how you handled them. Ask yourself: what have I learned and what will I do differently next time?
3. Reflect on what challenges you are most likely to face in your forthcoming career transition.
4. Look at the resources you have to meet those challenges and how you can use them to prepare.
5. Look at your affirmations!

REFLECTION

If there is one thing that you can work on to improve your career satisfaction, it is to believe in yourself and in your ability to succeed in whatever you want to achieve. Believing in yourself colours your attitude and your behaviour in every situation related to your career development. Every conversation you have with someone who can influence or affect your career then sends the subliminal message that you are competent and will achieve, and that message is clearly heard and understood by your audience. Confidence is empowering and infectious. How can I believe in the future of someone who does not believe in herself? Your will to succeed gets a boost when you grow in self-confidence. Those of you who suffer from impostor syndrome find it a constant battle to present a confident exterior that diverges from how you are feeling inside, and that is exhausting. Which is why it is worthwhile trying to overcome those feelings of inadequacy. Working on yourself to increase your self-confidence will enable you to be more relaxed and paradoxically achieve more.

CONCLUSION –
CHANGE IS YOUR CHOICE

Transition has its root in the Latin word *trans*, which means from one place to another, across, beyond, or through. A dear friend of mine once mentioned how she always felt unsettled once she had called a minicab; although she sat patiently enough waiting for it to arrive, she felt quite literally neither here nor there. She had not really left home, nor had she arrived at the place she wanted to be. Many of us will recognise that feeling of not being in the right place but don't quite know how or where to start when it comes to making that vital shift we so desire to make. It is my hope that this book has armed you with some tools to start identifying what that 'right place' is for you and moving towards it.

The gig economy and agile working – and therefore continual change and transitions – are here to stay. The Covid-19 pandemic only intensified a trend that had begun much earlier. Many women had wanted more flexibility and choice in their working hours and, although companies are still working out what this shift in work formats will mean in the long term and how to create hybrid working arrangements that benefit organisations and employees alike, we will definitely see more employment opportunities on a more flexible basis in the future. More people will be able to work from home at hours to suit themselves, joining virtual meetings with colleagues all over the world.

DOI: 10.4324/9781003353720-21

For many women, a hybrid working arrangement where they can work in the office for a few hours a day or a couple of days a week, creating time and space to devote to the family and other pursuits, will be welcome. Instead of a work–life balance, we can aim for a work–life mix. Transitioning from one project, job, or team to the next is also something we will need to do far more often than we were traditionally accustomed to doing.

All of this means that we need to prepare even more rigorously for constant change and for multiple career transitions. We need to learn to cultivate skills and awareness which will allow us to 'work the system', so to speak, and make use of its advantages such as working from home, flexi-time, and agile working.

It will be important not to lose sight of your career momentum in the midst of these changes and to remain visible and present, even when you are not in the office 9–5. Keeping in touch with colleagues and the boss and finding ways to network virtually will be key.

Similarly, agile working has become even more prominent where workers are assigned to small-scale projects and, once a project has been completed, move on to the next project and to (usually) a different set of co-workers and team leader, thus creating 'agile teams'. The rapid-moving tech industry has been key in influencing other industries to adopt this working pattern; standard-bearers like Google pride themselves on the way in which the agile working style is more productive than the traditional way of working. They argue that employees are more efficient, more creative, and more content.

This way of working will not be new for people in some professions. Musicians, for example, rarely experience the luxury of having a single employer for any stretch of time. The majority of professional musicians flit from one gig to the next, researching, practising, rehearsing, performing, and then moving on to the next project, which might be the next performance, or a recording, or a teaching assignment, or collaboration with a festival. Most musicians belong to more than one group, ensemble, or orchestra and are, to all intents and purposes, self-employed, hiring out their labour to several employers.

So, when considering what's next for you – whatever your existing working scenario might be – it is all the more important to be very clear about what you want and what suits you, to be adaptable, and to recognise that you always have a choice.

Awareness of your values, self-confidence, decision-making ability, resilience, supportive relationships, and self-reflection are all the more important in the agile working economy. If you are strong in your sense of self, you will rise to the challenge of a career transition and embrace the changing tide while also ensuring that that tide stays in line with your own goals, values, and progression aspirations.

All that remains to be said is that transitions are part of life; we can learn to look forward to them and all that they will bring. Take the insights in this book and use the tools from the self-reflection journal entries and the toolkit to prepare for the career transitions that will come your way so that when they arrive you know *exactly* what to do.

I hope that from the guidelines in this book, the inspiring stories of the women you have met and with the aid of the tools and exercises for reflection and action, you have gained an insight into both why it is important to nurture your career and also how to do so. Remember to reach out for support along the way, look to mentors in your life and in the wider world, and to learn from those around you. But above all, believe in yourself.

Transitions are part of life; we can learn to look forward to them.

TOOLKIT

IDENTITY

My values

Rank these values according to their importance in regard to your work choices. Note any additional values that are important to you.

Values for the role of work in my life	Not at all important	Important	Very important
Professional status			
Financial gain			
Serving the community			
Stability/security			
Independence			
Adventure			
Flexibility			
Gender equity			
Work-life balance			
Recognition			

Now take a look at the second kind of values around how organisations are run.

Values for the working environment	Not at all important	Important	Very important
An ethical culture based on integrity			
Diverse and inclusive			
Non-hierarchical			
Strong team spirit			
Flexible working			
Being in charge of my work and time			
Focused talent development			
A caring and psychologically 'safe' work environment			
Emphasis on innovation and creative thinking			
Strong workforce representation			

Now have a think about these questions.

1. Are you already living and working in a way which honours the things you value?
2. How can you add more of what you value to your work and to your life?
3. What do you need to change in order to fulfil your sense of self?

These are the questions that drive change in our lives. When you are considering a career move, try to find out what values drive the organisation you are planning to join and whether they match your own.

My success stories

Take several sheets of paper and mark each into two columns, headed as follows:

What I did	My success

I have found that thoughts flow particularly well with pen (or pencil) and paper, but if you prefer to do this exercise on a screen, please feel free to do so.

Think back over your life and remember some moments when you felt proud of what you had achieved, or someone else acknowledged your achievement or contribution. Choose a mixture from both professional and private life, and semi-professional, e.g. as captain of the swimming team or as organiser of a local community petition. What did you do at university that made you feel proud? What have you accomplished in your professional career so far? What were the highlights? When do you feel most in your comfort zone and confident about what you are doing or contributing?

Take your time to do this exercise. You may want to do it over a few days as you begin to remember your success stories.

What I did: Use as much space as you need. Make some notes about the example. What was the context? Who was involved? What did you set out to do? What did you do? Be sure to include any challenges or problems that you set out to solve.
My success: Why do you consider this story a success story? What did you achieve? Why were you satisfied with your achievement? Did you meet a personal challenge, or overcome a previous hurdle? Did other people recognise your success?

Take a moment to feel proud about your successes. It is really important to stop and realise just how much you have already achieved and celebrate this!

My transferable skills

Transferable skills are the skills and competencies that must be used in every kind of work context in addition to the professional skills that are directly related to the content of the job, such as accounting skills, legal know-how, supply chain knowledge, etc.

Look back to your past success stories and, using the activity below, identify which of the transferable skills in your examples contributed to your success. Draw on the success stories used in the previous activity.

1. Make a note of your top transferable skills
2. Where are you already using them in your current job?
3. In which kind of position could you include them more frequently? Look out for any opportunities to introduce them in your work. For example, if one of your top strengths is negotiating, then see how you could work with clients or with other teams in situations where negotiating skill is required.
4. Think about a career transition where you could make more use of your top transferable skills. For example, if business acumen, client relations, and strategic thinking are among your top skills, you might like to consider going independent, or at least seeking a professional context where you can make more use of these skills.
5. Which transferable skills might you need to strengthen for your next career move? How will you do that? Identify ways and opportunities to improve in preparation for your next career move.

	Success story 1	*Success story 2*	*Success story 3*	*Success story 4*
Communication – listening/ understanding, negotiating				
Teaching, coaching, mentoring				
Presenting/speaking to a group				
Being innovative				

Planning and organising				
Cultural sensitivity				
Time management				
Diplomacy/tact				
Resilience/perseverance				
Team spirit – bringing people together				
Motivating and inspiring others				
Strategic thinking				
Practical problem-solving				
Decision-making				
Business acumen				

My profile

1. Begin with your professional expertise. What is your area of competence (publishing, banking, HR, law, etc.)?
2. Now narrow that down to be more specific about your very particular areas of knowledge – what are you the go-to person for in your firm? What makes you different from all the other accountants or lawyers or project managers?
3. Ask as many people as you like (minimum five) to give you three adjectives that describe you. Ask colleagues, ex-colleagues, managers, coaches, and also friends.
4. Write your professional profile in no more than five lines highlighting your area of expertise and your experience. If you were a can of soup, what would the label say about you?

My interests

What are you really interested in doing? Now is the time to lay the groundwork for including more of what really interests you in your work.

1. Brainstorm or doodle everything that interests you including not only work-related activities but also things that currently have nothing to do with your work.

2. Separate out the things that are strictly personal, such as your family.

3. Now look again and identify the activities that you would like to do more of in your next career move. Allow yourself to think outside of the box – be brave! These could include:

    a. Areas that you could include in your current work context but perhaps in a different role, such as taking on a managerial role, working more with clients, negotiating, etc.

    b. New activities or areas that are different from what you do currently but that you would like to explore.

    c. Different contexts, such as working independently, but still doing the kind of work you do currently.

4. Identify what really interests you – what would you be excited to do next?

REALITY

Columns of opportunity

The columns of opportunity table is a structured way of collecting your ideas about where you would like to work: the kind of work you want to do, the type, size, and location of the organisation you would like to work in, and any special thoughts you have.

1. Create your own columns of opportunity – 4–6 columns is a good number.

Opportunities	1	2	3	4
My area of expertise				
My wished focus, e.g. small projects				
My target context				
My desired type of employment				
My desired location				
Additional thoughts				

Your columns are not set in stone – you can add or take away at any time as your research progresses. The main thing is to proactively and methodically do your research into what is available that matches your profile and interests.

Here is an example. Andrea's expertise was in marketing, but she wanted to move into the context of healthcare. These are her columns of opportunity.

Opportunities		*1*	*2*	*3*	*4*
My area of expertise	Marketing/ branding	Healthcare institutions/ private hospitals	Alternative medicine companies	Pharmaceutical companies	Gyms/ physio institutes
My wished focus	Small projects				
My target context	Healthcare				
My desired type of employment	Small/ medium-sized (SME)				
My desired location	Bristol/ West country				
Additional thoughts	Must match my values				

2. The next step is to research potential employers that match the criteria with all the resources available to you, on the internet, through your network, in industry associations, forums, etc., and insert the names of these organisations and companies into your table.

3. Methodically research these potential places of employment and find out as much as you can about them. Reach out to talk to people at these organisations to get more information.

4. As you do your research, you will begin to see a clear picture of which companies you would like to work for and what you could offer them. You will also realise where you do **not** want to work – which is also valuable!

Going independent – a skills and mindset checklist

The following skills and mindset factors are especially useful for being an independent, self-employed woman, whether as a consultant or as a business owner. Check the ones you already have and make a note of those you need to develop.

Skill/Mindset	Check	Develop
Thinking strategically and planning		
Hard-working		
Resilience and determination		
Organising		
Business acumen and know-how		
Financial know-how and budgeting		
Time management		
People skills		
Decision-making		
Risk management		

Visualisation exercises

Visualisation exercises are a great way of tapping into your unconscious to help you choose your next career move. They work in addition to the practical research you do as they allow you to realise and accept how you feel.

Exercise 1

1. Find a quiet space and close your eyes. Imagine yourself in a job where you feel fulfilled. Just allow a picture to float to the surface.

What do you see? Where are you? What are you doing? Who are the people with you? How do you feel? Afterwards, make a few notes in your journal about what you saw and how you felt.

2. In your visualisation, watch yourself succeeding in the new job. See how you handle the people and the situation you are in.

Exercise 2

1. Create a visual mood board of your aspirations. Ideally, this is an actual board or space on your wall where you can fix sticky notes and pictures, memos and doodles, whatever comes to hand that you find and that resonates with you while you are thinking about what kind of work you would like to do. Alternatively, you can do this on your computer using a mood board tool such as Pinterest.

2. Don't hold back with the details! The more detail you have in your visual mood board the closer, more energised, and positive you will feel about achieving that next career move.

My network map

Networking is a key activity at all stages of your career transition. You need to reach out to the people in your network for information about potential opportunities, what suggestions they have, additional contacts for more information, for support, and… and… and! Your network is one of the most important resources you have. And you can grow your network constantly!

1. Create a map of your network with yourself in the middle with contacts around you.

2. Reflect on what support you need at the moment – is it information, advice, suggestions, contacts,….?

3. Identify the contacts who could provide what you need. If you see gaps in your network map which need filling, make a note of how you could potentially fill them.

4. Ask the people in your network map if they can put you in touch with someone who can give you the kind of information/ advice you are looking for.

5. Use your social networks and professional and alumni associations to search for the right person.

6. Revisit your network map regularly to add new contacts.
7. When you have a professional conversation with someone, always ask if they can recommend someone else to whom you could talk. Make your network grow effectively!

Notice that you are not necessarily asking anyone for a job. You are simply using your network to gather information on a regular and ad hoc basis. At the same time, you are strengthening the bonds of your network and signalling that you are there for others, too, when they need you. Networking is a two-way activity.

PRESENTATION

My job search – practical steps

How to write your CV

Your CV is a complete presentation of your work experience, your education and academic qualifications, and your key (i.e. relevant) skills and competencies. Many organisations have an online CV template for you to fill in. If not, you can use the Europass, created as a standardised template application throughout the EU.

There are two main CV formats: chronological and functional. If your CV is fairly long, consider using the functional format in which you use your areas of competence, such as project management, as headings, and then list the relevant work under the headings. The layout you use is up to you (if there is no template) and you will find many on offer on the internet; just make sure it is easy to read and not too 'busy'.

Your CV is a marketing tool. You should make the most of your relevant skills and experience to demonstrate you are highly suitable for the position that you are applying for. Use the key words from the vacancy announcement in your CV. Most employers and recruiters do an electronic key word search to scan for suitable candidates. Do not be afraid to 'sell' yourself in your CV.

Your CV is a living document; although you and your expertise and experience remain the same, you will need to adapt your CV to highlight what the recruiter is looking for in a particular job. Do not rely on a one-size-fits-all CV — make it an expression of what the recruiter needs. Always spellcheck your CV for typos. You need to make a good impression!

Name	Put the first name you normally use and your family name
Photo	You can include a photo
Address	Use a current home address
Email	Use your personal email address
Telephone	Include country code if applying globally
Internet	LinkedIn, your own website if you have one, especially if you are an independent (consultant, etc.)
Key profile	Highlight in three or four sentences your expertise and your key experience that matches the kind of position you are looking for or applying to. This is your opening sales pitch; make it captivating.
Skills and competencies	Include technology you are familiar with. Include data and values to support the text. Consider including attributes colleagues have mentioned.
Work history	Job title, company, position, and dates. Highlight in each job the skills you used. Include key achievements with results.
Qualifications/ Education/ Training	Include academic qualifications and relevant training. For a scientific/research/academic position include a relevant publications list.
Interests	Include some interests if they support your application. Show your commitment to the sector or your interest in the organisation's cause, perhaps in volunteering or pro bono work.

Sample CV: Chronological

Some recruiters, especially in the US, ask for a one-page summary as a CV or résumé. Here, you need to be strategic and extract from your full CV the information that is going to make you stand out from the crowd. Highlight your skills and experience that are most relevant to the position. Anything else is redundant.

How to write a cover letter

Your cover letter is your opportunity to stand out from all the other applicants. It describes why you are interested in the position and why you are a good match. Use it to convey more about yourself than is stated in the CV. It should be brief, 4–5 paragraphs, if possible, on one A4 page. The cover letter also provides a sample of your writing skills. Pay attention to spelling, grammar, and style.

Letter structure

1. Open with a statement of interest in one short paragraph. Explain why you are interested in the position and state here already in one phrase what makes you a suitable match.
2. Summarise your qualifications, competencies, skills, and experience in 2–3 paragraphs. Describe how your experience and skills match the requirements for the position. A good method is to start from the vacancy announcement: describe your experience not in chronological form but related to the requirements. The recruiter can read your employment history in your CV, so there is no need to repeat it here.
3. As necessary, include one short paragraph on your academic and technical qualifications as required in the advertisement.
4. Close with a brief overview of your suitability for the position and your understanding of the organisation/company and – most important – what you feel you could contribute to the success of the office or department.

Points to watch out for

1. Always draft in word processing software before pasting the cover letter into an online application.

2. Spellcheck and proofread.
3. Be positive and professional.
4. Show confidence in yourself.
5. Save a copy for yourself.

How to write a letter of interest

The letter of interest is like a cover letter but instead of applying for a specific position, you are expressing your interest in working for the organisation. If you can use your network or an event you have attended to get the name of someone who would have some influence or authority, preferably someone in a department where you would like to work, then address your letter to that person. If possible, refer to a mutual contact (who has ideally already contacted this person and given them a heads-up about you!). This is networking at its most useful.

Start by explaining what interests you about the company/organisation and how you think you would add value to their work. Try to use a 'hook' to capture the attention of the person you are writing to, such as referring to an article about the company or even a blog they have written; if a specific issue or challenge is mentioned, see if you can refer to that as a problem you have some experience in solving.

Write a short summary of your key expertise and experience, highlighting the skills and competencies that would be particularly relevant for the kind of work the department does and the challenges they face.

Request a brief meeting and say you will follow up with a phone call.

Nothing ventured, nothing gained!

How to prepare for interview – 11 tips

Everybody needs to prepare well for an interview. You can't just wing it.

1. Research the organisation. Find out as much as you can about who they are and what they do, where they operate, their successes, and their challenges.

   Why? A favourite question from interviewers runs on the lines of: 'Why do you want to work for us?' Or even: 'What do you know about Company X?'

2. Find out as much as possible about the job itself. Try to get more information than what is in the job advertisement. You can try and talk to the hiring manager, to the HR recruiter, and, if you have an inside track, to someone in the organisation.

   Why? Additional information about the job can be very useful in your answers. You will recognise when a question touches on something that is considered important. You will be prepared to talk about that subject and you will therefore look like less of an outsider.

3. Find out how the interview will be conducted. Usually, this is clearly stated in the invitation to interview. Will you be asked 'behavioural' questions? Are you required to give a presentation about a specific subject? Prepare well and leave time for questions and answers.

   Why? This is vital information for you to be able to prepare correctly. Behavioural interviewing questions are structured around so-called competencies and ask for examples of your past behaviour in professional circumstances. Make sure to find out whether the interview will be based on the organisation's competency framework. Some interviews include 'scenarios' in which the kind of situation you would face in the position is outlined to you and you are asked for your thoughts on how you would handle it: prepare for such scenarios.

4. Be prepared for 'out-of-the-box' questions such as: 'What would you do with a million pounds?' This is a great opportunity for you to show what you are passionate about and how you would use a large sum of money. If possible, include something that has some connection with what the company does or with a pressing social issue.

   Why? Interviewers like to test a candidate's agility to respond to unexpected questions. It's a sign of flexible thinking and at the same time demonstrates an ability to stay focused on the topic in hand.

5. Find out who will interview you. Will it be one person or two, or a panel? If possible, get their names or at least their positions and do your research on them.

   Why? Knowing in advance what position the interviewers hold and some information about their background means you can get an idea of what things they might ask you about.

6. Practise talking about your expertise, your knowledge, and your experience.

    Why? We very rarely talk about ourselves in the way that is expected at interview, and some of us are not comfortable when we have to do so. This is the one situation where you have to present yourself in your best light and do so in a confident and articulate manner. Practise with a friend, your partner, or a coach, or record a video of yourself.

7. Plan your journey if you are invited to attend in person. Make sure you know where you are going and how long it takes to get there.

    Why? There is really nothing worse than arriving late or just in time but hot and flustered to an interview. If possible, do a dummy run. An address in London or Leeds may seem straightforward in the instructions and on Google Maps but in practice can be quite difficult to find. Time spent in reconnaissance is never wasted. Consider taking a taxi for the last part of the way so that you arrive calm, rested, and clean!

8. Look the part. Dress as though you already work at the company.

    Why? Although it is not true that interviewers decide within 20 seconds whether they want to offer you the job – as some rumours have it – first impressions are still important. This is another reason why a dummy run is a good idea. Watch the women going into the office. How are they dressed? Try to look as though you will fit in. Make sure your clothes are neat and clean, your hair is tidy, and your nails and makeup, if you use it, are perfect. Do not wear excessive makeup or perfume or large costume jewellery because it distracts the interviewers from what you are saying.

9. Prepare a short but informative answer to the question: 'Tell us about yourself'.

    Why? Some interviewers think this is a kind opening question and they are attempting to put you at your ease. In fact, of course, many people are uncomfortable with this question. Prepare your answer carefully, offering a summary of your key expertise which shows how you fit well for the position you are applying for. Incorporate your profile statement! The question may vary, such as: 'What makes you uniquely suitable for this position?'

Do not attempt to give a résumé of your career. Explain why you would love to work for the organisation and what you feel you can contribute to their success; concentrate on your most relevant key skills and know-how. One minute is long enough for an answer to this question.

Practise with a friend or partner or by recording a video of yourself.

10. Prepare some questions for the interviewers.

Why? Most interviewers ask at the end of the interview whether you have any questions, and you should have one or two questions ready. Use the opportunity to show you have researched the organisation and/or the potential challenges of the job and ask intelligently about the tasks facing the new incumbent of the position.

11. Relax!

Try to relax before the interview by using breathing techniques and relaxation exercises. If you know you are particularly prone to interview nerves, ask yourself why this is so; does the situation take you back to tests at school? If so, remind yourself that then you were young but now you are an experienced professional. Remember that this is not a test situation but a conversation where the interviewers are genuinely interested in you and their purpose is not to mark you up or down but to see whether you are the person they are looking for to fill the position; which is exactly your purpose, too. Remember you have a lot to offer. Put the past behind you; that was then, this is now.

BUILDING CONFIDENCE

How to build self-confidence

Getting positive feedback

1. Ask 5–6 people, preferably a mix of friends and colleagues, to give you positive feedback by making brief notes on 2–3 situations when you showed special competence in something. Ask them to identify the skills or abilities you demonstrated.

2. Go back to your success stories and strengths that you listed in Part 1 and compare the strengths that others identified with the ones you see in yourself. Are they different or the same? Are there additional strengths you had not thought of?

Recognising my achievements

1. Make a list of your key achievements in life – this could be gaining qualifications, success in a job role, positive feedback from friends or colleagues, contributions to your local community or charities, or perhaps progress with a hobby.
2. Be quite specific about what makes that event an achievement and pinpoint your abilities and talents that helped you achieve what you did.
3. Take a moment to reflect on and honour your achievements and the talents that underpin them.

Daily affirmations

Choose an affirmation that speaks to you at that moment. Try to choose your affirmation at the start of your day during a quiet moment alone. Reinforce your affirmation by saying it aloud several times. You can choose the same affirmation for several days or change your affirmation whenever you like. Repeat your affirmation several times throughout the day.

1. I am grounded and confident
2. I am aware of my abilities
3. I meet the day's challenges in a positive way
4. There are no blocks that I can't overcome
5. I am worthy of having the job I want
6. I can achieve whatever I want
7. All I need is within me
8. I release anything that does not serve me
9. I draw on my strengths
10. Everything is possible
11. I can do this
12. Every day brings me closer to my career goal

I am good enough

Striving to do the best you can at the time, perhaps better than last time, is a constructive attitude; striving to be perfect in everything, on the other hand, can actually be destructive because you fail to put things into perspective. The concept of 'I am good enough' is useful because it inspires us to step up to a challenge and convince ourselves that we do have what it takes to meet that challenge. At the same time, we do not need to feel that we are the best in the world.

I am good enough

1. Consider the career transition you have in mind and write down what would be necessary to make that transition.
2. When you have your list, take a good look at everything and tick off every point where you know you have the skills and qualities required or what you believe you could handle with some learning time.
3. How many points have you ticked? More than half? Three quarters? Nearly everything? As long as you have ticked the majority of points you are good enough. Let that thought sink in.

I am good enough and do not need to be perfect

1. Write down one of your current goals or projects and define what success will look like when you have finished.
2. Adjust the success criteria to represent what you could accept as good enough but not perfect.
3. When you have accomplished this, accept it as your success.

How to become more resilient

1. Consider how resilient you are on a scale of 1–10 where 1 is not resilient at all and 10 is very resilient, where you are able to cope with anything that comes your way. Coping means that you are mentally prepared to say 'I can overcome this challenge'.
2. Find some examples of when you faced a challenge and remember how you handled them. Ask yourself: what have I learned and what will I do differently next time?
3. Reflect on what challenges you are most likely to face in your forthcoming career transition.
4. Look at the resources you have that will help you meet those challenges and how you can use them to prepare.
5. Look at your affirmations!

ACCLIMATISATION – FINDING MY FEET IN THE NEW ENVIRONMENT

Putting myself in another's shoes exercises

When you are acclimatising to your new workplace, sometimes what is required of you or how a new colleague behaves may seem strange. So, it can be helpful to do one of the following exercises and see things from another perspective.

Sitting in their place

1. Place two chairs a little distance apart and sit in one. This is your place. From where you are sitting, think about your new work-place and the people you interact with. Who do you need to know more about? It could be a colleague or your manager or a client. Look at the other chair. That chair is that person's place.

2. What do you feel about that person when you look at that chair? What do you know about them? What more would you like to know? What do you feel is your relationship?

3. Now stand up from your place, move to the other chair, and sit down in the other person's place. How does it feel? What wishes or concerns do you notice? Now, look at the other chair (= your place). What feelings do you have about the person who sits in that place (= you)? What would you like to know?

4. Stand up and move back to your place. Sit in your chair. Reflect on what you have learned about the other person. Has anything changed in your view of them? What would you like to say to them? Will you behave differently towards them? What questions might you ask them?

5. Stand up and step to one side. Look at the two chairs and ask yourself from an outsider's perspective what could or needs to change about the relationship.

6. Make a few notes about what you have learned and what action steps you are going to take.

Moving in space (This and other useful exercises can be found in *Insights in Space* by James Lawley and Marian Way (Fareham, Cedar Group 2017))

1. Put the names of the people in your new job that you interact with most on sticky notes or pieces of paper. Arrange the sticky

    notes on the floor around you, approximately in the kind of distance that you feel there is between you and them. This does not need to be exact.

2. Take up a position in the room where you feel that you are in relation to your colleagues.

3. Move to the first (closest) person's sticky note. Pick it up off the floor and reflect on that person and your relationship with them. Put yourself in that person's shoes mentally. How do they feel about you and other colleagues? What does work look like from where they are? Make a few notes on the sticky note. You do not need to **know** anything special to do this activity, just consider how it feels to be that person.

4. Move to the next person's sticky note and repeat the reflection. Again, make a few notes.

5. Move around until you have stood in every place and reflected on how your work and colleagues look from each position. Make a few notes in your journal about the exercise. How will your reflections help you in your transition?

Building trust

Moving into a new job requires that you build mutual trust. Your new colleagues need to build trust in you, and you need to build up a sense that you can trust them. Trust has been shown to be the primary factor in good working relationships and, consequently, good work, and it is essential for a successful career transition.

    Trust is built on two different levels: a fast level and a slower, deeper level, based on the following criteria (adapted from Oxfam GB (2007)).

How to build trust fast

1. I am competent in my professional activities
2. I share information
3. I am honest and truthful and act with integrity
4. I trust others and I give people the benefit of the doubt

How to build deeper trust

1. I notice where I share a background, values, interests, etc. with colleagues
2. I am concerned about others' welfare
3. I am consistent in my approach and reliable
4. I have nothing to fear (the concept of psychological safety)
5. I include others in outside work activities
6. I share some personal things about myself

These are mutual criteria; in the interests of building trust we hope that colleagues will behave similarly, but when you are the new person in the mix, you have to make a start.

Preparing for an initial meeting with my new manager

Plan your initial meeting with your new manager meticulously. You need to find out how they work and how they want you to work with them.

1. Summarise for yourself what you already know
2. Prepare a list of questions
   a. What are your work priorities?
   b. How often does the manager want an update on your progress, any substantive changes, unexpected developments and results, etc.?
   c. How would your manager like you to communicate with them (email, WhatsApp, face-to-face, etc.)?
   d. Who in the team should you work most closely with; is there a 'work buddy' system, if not, could you nevertheless have one colleague to whom you could turn for support?
   e. How often do team meetings take place, and how are they conducted?
   f. How can you best support your manager/the team?
   g. What is most important for you to learn/develop first?
3. Request a meeting after a couple of months to discuss your progress and career development options. At that meeting, you can identify a special assignment to develop a skill.

Preparing for first meetings with my team as a new manager myself

Initial meetings with your team members are an important opportunity to make a first impression and to begin to pick up information about the individuals and about the team as a whole, so set up individual meetings as well as team meetings to begin to get to know each of them on a one-to-one basis. A successful meeting is one where your team member talks more than you do!

1. Before the individual meetings, find out as much as you can about each team member from past evaluations, work submitted, results, etc.
2. Schedule the meeting either face-to-face or virtually with enough time for the conversation; be present and engaged (turn off email and phone alerts).
3. Have a basic plan for the meeting and ask the following kind of questions:
   a. What does your work plan look like now?
   b. Are there any areas of work/tasks/types of assignments which you particularly enjoy doing?
   c. What areas would you like to do more of?
   d. How do you see the team working together?
   e. Do you have any difficulties you would like to share with me?
   f. Do you have any ideas on improving our work?
   g. Is there anything else you would like me to know?

Say that you hope you will work well together and that they can always come to you with any concerns and with any good ideas.

Guidelines for a mentoring relationship

1. Consider what you would like the goal of mentoring to be. Identify the topic or areas in which you would like help and support from your mentor from the list below.
   a. Insight into the organisation
   b. Overview of the industry/field
   c. Introductions to people in/outside the organisation

    d.   Strategic career planning

    e.   Help with specific, career-related issues, e.g. teamwork competence, difficulties with a supervisor, managerial skills

2. Choose as your mentor someone whom you respect and trust, and who will be able to help you in the areas you have identified as your goals for mentoring.

3. Lay down the guidelines for the mentoring relationship in writing: how long the relationship will last, frequency, length, and place of meetings, and your methods of communicating with each other. This agreement will help to put the relationship on a formal footing.

4. A mentoring relationship normally lasts a year. This gives time for the relationship to develop and be productive. You should aim to meet approximately once a month or every six weeks if possible, face-to-face or virtually. Regular meetings are the most useful.

5. At the first meeting, together with your mentor choose one topic or area to focus on for the first three months. You may like to continue with the same topic after that time or choose another for the next three months.

6. It is always possible to bring up an urgent matter, but generally speaking, try to stay focused on the chosen topics.

7. Your mentor will suggest tasks or assignments for you to complete between meetings which will consolidate what has been discussed. These can be of a practical nature, e.g. giving a presentation, or you might be asked to do some research on a topic. Ask your mentor to set challenging tasks. You want to grow over the year.

8. After about six months or halfway through the agreed mentoring time, review your progress and the relationship. Are you getting what you want out of it? Address any issues openly.

At the end of the year, review together what has been accomplished.

Mapping my new team

In this activity, you will create a three-dimensional mind map of your new team as you perceive the working relationships to be at the moment and then see what you would like to change. When you do the exercise, use your feelings as much as your thoughts. This is a very powerful and useful exercise as you gain a deeper level of understanding about your new team and how you fit in.

1. Take several small objects that you have easily to hand such as coloured pencils, paperclips, erasers, paperweights, or eggcups and small coffee cups. Each object represents a colleague in your new team. Also, choose an object to represent yourself.
2. Place yourself on the (cleared) table and then place the other people around you. Think and try to feel where the objects should stand. This will be influenced by their relationship to you.
3. Take a good look at the three-dimensional map of your team. Who is facing towards you and who is facing away? What clusters of people do you notice? Who is most distant? Who is closest?
4. Who would you like to get closer to? Who needs to move? Move the objects into positions that you feel are the desirable positions.
5. Reflect on how you can make these shifts in position happen in real life. What do you need to do?

ME AT WORK

My work style

It is really helpful to become aware of your work style as we usually just accept that's the way it is for everyone – until we meet a colleague who works very differently. Different is not better or worse – it's just different, and different work styles can often complement each other very well.

Reflect on the following opposites. Where does your work style fit?

1. I use lists to prioritise my work/I am flexible about when I do things
2. I like to work things out on my own/I prefer to brainstorm ideas in a group

3. I complete work quickly/I like to take my time and be thorough
4. I am detail-oriented/I always try to see the big picture
5. I plan everything/I like to leave room for the unexpected to happen
6. I work well under pressure/I don't like stress
7. I am very methodical/I get ideas from everywhere
8. I'm a workaholic/I need downtime to regenerate

Communication checklist

1. Plan your communication. What do you want to get out of the conversation? What should be different at the end?
2. What do you think the other person wants to get out of the conversation? How interested are they in having the conversation? How will you make them interested? What's in it for them?
3. Plan the right time, place, and mode for the conversation.
4. Consider the other person's background, their culture, professional situation, and also their personal context.
5. Pick the person up from where they are standing; bring them closer to you and do not expect them to take the first step. Explain what's in it for them.
6. Practise really listening; then play back what you think you have heard.
7. Listen between 'the lines'.
8. Consider what language the other person speaks: English (native or not)…, IT…, business…., scientific…, marketing,…., etc.
9. Use the other person's language as far as possible to help them feel you understand them better.
10. Have a (mental) checklist of the points you want to get across and how you want the conversation to go (talking points).
11. Stay focused on the topic of the conversation without digressing.
12. Check that the other person has understood you by asking them to paraphrase or summarise what they heard you say.
13. Also check back that you have understood your partner.

14. At the end of the conversation summarise what you have agreed (action points).

Receiving feedback

1. Ask for feedback about the way you handled a situation and analyse that feedback objectively.
2. When you receive feedback, reflect on how it made you feel, then separate the emotion from the message.
3. Reflect on what you can learn from the feedback for the future.
4. Go back over similar situations and reflect on what you could have done differently; then be on the lookout for situations to put your insights into practice.

How to gain a good reputation and get yourself noticed

Just doing good work, even superb work, is not enough to ensure your career progression in an organisation. It is just the foundation. Your work has to be noticed by the right people and you need to build a good reputation to move forward.

1. Reflect on whose opinion counts in your organisation. Whose orbit do you need to be in to be noticed as an employee with a future?
2. Make a list of the people you work with, then highlight those who should know about the results you achieve.
3. Consider who else should know about your achievements. This could be a manager at a higher level in the same department or someone with influence in a different part of the company.
4. Identify ways to become visible to the people who can support you in your career development. Here are some ideas:
   a. keep your manager informed about your achievements
   b. post interesting content on the internal website
   c. take part in a high-visibility project
   d. volunteer for a special assignment
   e. become the focal point for an interest group
   f. put forward an innovative suggestion
   g. create an action group

h. get on the new ideas committee if your organisation has one, and if not see if you could organise one
i. choose a mentor in a department where you see potential for your career growth.

REFERENCES

TOOLKIT

Oxfam GB. (2007) *Building Trust in Diverse Teams: The toolkit for emergency response*. https://policy-practice.oxfam.org/resources/building-trust-in-diverse-teams-the-toolkit-for-emergency-response-115413/

PART 1

American Express. (2019) *State of the Women-Owned Businesses Report.* https://s1.q4cdn.com/692158879/files/doc_library/file/2019-state-of-women-owned-businesses-report.pdf

Correa, Guillermina. (2020) UENI's *2020 Report on Gender and Small Business.* Updated 15 July 2021. UENI. https://ueni.com/blog/report-gender-small-business-female/

Yordanova, Inna. (2019) *Women in Self-Employment.* IPSE. https://www.ipse.co.uk/policy/research/women-in-self-employment/women-in-self-employment.html

Dweck, C. S. (2006) *Mindset: The New Psychology of Success.* New York: Random House Publishing Group.

PART 3

The Behavioural Insights Team. (2019) *Women only apply for jobs when 100% qualified. Fact or fake news?* Blog post, 20 November. https://www.bi.team/blogs/women-only-apply-for-jobs-when-100-qualified-fact-or-fake-news/

Hewlett Packard. (2014) Internal report. Cited in: Mohr, Tara Sophia. (2014) *Why Women Don't Apply for Jobs Unless They're 100% Qualified.* Harvard Business Review. https://hbr.org/2014/08/why-women-dont-apply-for-jobs-unless-theyre-100-qualified

The Hub Events. (2019) *Impostor Syndrome Survey Results.* https://www.thehubevents.com/resources/impostor-syndrome-survey-results

Leadem, Rose. (2017) *12 Leaders, Entrepreneurs and Celebrities Who Have Struggled With Imposter Syndrome.* Entrepreneur.com. https://www.entrepreneur.com/slideshow/304273

Obama, Michelle. (2018) *Becoming.* New York: Viking Press.

FURTHER READING

Barsh, J., & Yee, L. (2011, April). Unlocking the Full Potential of Women in the US Economy. http://www.mckinsey.com/Client_Service/Organization/Latest_thinking/Unlocking_the_full_potential.aspx

Braun Levine, S. (2005). *Inventing The Rest of Our Lives*. New York: Penguin.

Csikszentmihalyi, M. (1990). *Flow. The Psychology of Optimal Experience*. New York: HarperCollins.

Devine Brigid Francis, N. F. (2021, March 2). Women and the Economy. ww.parliament.uk/commons-library.

Dweck, C. S. (2006). *Mindset: The New Psychology of Success*. New York: Random House Publishing Group.

Eisold, K. (2009). *What You Don't Know You Know*. New York: Other Press.

Fletcher, J. K. (2001). *Disappearing Acts. Gender, Power, and Relational Practice at Work*. Cambridge, MA: MIT Press.

French, R. & Simpson, P. (2014). *Attention, Cooperation, Purpose: An Approach to Working in Groups Using Insights from Wilfred Bion*. London: Karnac.

Furnham, A. (2005). The Psychology of Behaviour at Work. The Individual in the Organization, 2nd ed. Hove: Psychology Press.

Hirschhorn, L. (1988). *The Workplace Within: Psychodynamics of Organizational Life*. Cambridge, MA: MIT Press.

Holmes, J. (2006). *Gendered Talk at Work*. Oxford: Blackwell.

Jeffers, S. (2011). *Feel The Fear and Do It Anyway*. London: Arrow Books, Random House.

Kabat-Zinn, J. (2012). *Mindfulness for Beginners: Reclaiming the Present Moment - and Your Life*. Boulder, CO: Sounds True.

Kahnemann, D. (2011). *Thinking, Fast and Slow*. New York: Farrar, Straus and Giroux.

Kay, K. and Shipman, C. (2014). *The Confidence Code*. New York: Harper Collins.

Lees, J. (2020). *How To Get a Job You Love*, 11th ed. London: OUP.

Lewis, S. (2011). *Positive Psychology at Work: How Positive Leadership and Appreciative Inquiry Create Inspiring Organizations*. Chichester: Wiley-Blackwell.

Obama, M. (2018). *Becoming*. Penguin Random House.

Obholzer, A., & Zagier Roberts, V. (eds.) (1994). *The Unconscious at Work*. Hove: Routledge.

Perez, C. C. (2019). *Invisible Women - Exposing Data Bias in a World Designed for Men*. London: Vintage.

Petty, R. (2014, March 12). *The Atlantic*. Retrieved September 9, 2014, from The Atlantic: www.theatlantic.com/features/archive/2014/04/the-confidence-gap/359815/

Salenbacher, H. (2013). *Creative Personal Branding*. Amsterdam: BIS.

Sandberg, S. (2013). *Lean In: Women, Work and the Will to Lead*. New York: Knopf.

Seligman, M. (2011). *Flourish: A New Understanding of Happiness and Well-Being - and How To Achieve Them*. New York: Hodder and Stoughton.

Syed, M. (2016). *Black Box Thinking*. London: John Murray.

Tirard, A., & Harbour-Lyell, C. (2017). *Disrupt Your Career: How to Navigate Uncharted Career Transitions and Thrive*. Lulu Publishing Services.

Tupper, H. E. (2020). *The Squiggly Career*. London: Penguin Random House.

Vallely, V. (2013). *Heels of Steel: How to Survive & Thrive in the Corporate World*. London: Panoma.

Wasylyshyn, K. (2014). *Destined To Lead: Executive Coaching and Lessons for Leadership Development*. New York: Palgrave Macmillan.

Watkins, M. D. (2013). *The First 90 Days: Proven Strategies for Getting Up to Speed Faster and Smarter*. Boston, MA: Harvard Business Review.

Wendleton, K. (2014). *Targeting a Great Career. (The Five O'Clock Club)*, 5th ed. New York: Cengage Learning.

INDEX

Printed in the United States
by Baker & Taylor Publisher Services